WITHDRAWN

B

BOOKS
FOR WARTIME

BERLIN DIARY
The Journal of a Foreign Correspondent
1934–1941
by William L. Shirer

DESIGN FOR POWER
by Frederick L. Schuman
maps by George D. Brodsky

OUR HAWAII
by Erna Fergusson

CRISIS IN THE PHILIPPINES
by Catherine Porter

JAPAN'S INDUSTRIAL STRENGTH
by Kate L. Mitchell

These are Borzoi Books, published by
ALFRED A. KNOPF

THE JAPANESE ENEMY

THE
JAPANESE
ENEMY

HIS POWER AND
HIS VULNERABILITY

BY

HUGH BYAS

NEW YORK · ALFRED A KNOPF · 1942

Manufactured in the United States of America
Published simultaneously in Canada by The Ryerson Press

Published February 16, 1942
Second Printing, February 1942
Third Printing, March 1942

"When the Mediterranean was the center of civilization the world's leaders were Greece and Rome. Now the scene has shifted to the Pacific, and Japan stands on the pivot of the world. We have opportunities given by heaven, advantages given by nature, and national unity."

—from a Japanese army pamphlet

THE AUTHOR EXPLAINS

In TRYING to get the news from Japan across to American readers a correspondent's perpetual difficulty is the difference between words and things. He uses the ordinary words of his trade—Emperor, Cabinet, constitution, legislature, dictator, and so on—and the reader does not know that the things they mean in Japan are not the things they mean anywhere else. Even the word "army" —how is the non-Japanese reader to understand that the army in Japan is not only a fighting force but a political force exercising a control over policy roughly comparable to that of a party with a permanent majority and the chief of the state in its pocket? How is he to know that this position is quite "constitutional" and that the results which flow from it are accepted by the Japanese people as normal? Or take the word "dictatorship." Japanese have often put to me a Socratic question they considered conclusive: "How can there be a dictatorship when there is no dictator?" The government of Japan is in fact at this moment (that is, during a state of war) a military dictatorship, but it is held in commission by the army and navy. The reason why no dictator has arisen is that political Japan is not a nation of individuals but a hive of bees working, buzzing, and fighting collectively in defense of the hive. Latterly I never used the term "public opinion" in messages from Japan though I had to report editorials in leading journals, comments by columnists, mass meetings, speeches, processions and demonstrations. Since the army launched Japan on a policy of aggression in 1931, these things have been but the instinctive buzzing of the swarm.

Behind a façade in modern style the Japanese system of government is still a Japanese structure—soft floors, silk cushions, opaque windows, dim alcoves, and sudden stenches. You see a constitution, a throne, a parliament, an electorate; high finance and big business; an army and navy; until yesterday you could see political parties and their machines; always the patriotic societies lurking in the darkness with dagger and bomb. Japan is ruled by a balance of groups in unstable equilibrium in which each of these plays a part. The part varies; when the theme is war, the army and navy have the stage and all the others carry spears. The only fixed principle—if it can be called a principle—is figurehead government. It can be seen through all the centuries of Japanese history and it prevails today. There is no fixed center of national power. The Japanese, who are always talking of national unity, have never been able to agree on the center of power. Their only center is the Emperor, a divine and powerless figurehead. It is their subconscious sense of his earthly weakness that causes the Japanese to claim divinity for their sovereign. Divinity treads on no one's toes. The system is fluid and unfinished, and that is the reason why we need not entirely despair of Japan.

This book is, in part, an effort to explain some of the hows and whys and becauses of those peculiarities. For its original impetus I am greatly indebted to a number of stimulating conversations with Dr. Brooks Emeny, Director of the Foreign Affairs Council, Cleveland, Ohio. In part it is a sermon on the too often forgotten text: "Despise not thine enemy." It examines the plea of economic necessity which Americans in good faith have sometimes made in extenuation of Japanese aggressiveness, and it squeezes some of the water out of the prospectus which has so often introduced Japan as a young nation driven wild by hardship and injustice.

CONTENTS

THE JAPANESE ENEMY

CHAPTER I

WAR CALCULATIONS

SUNDAY, DECEMBER 7 (*Cleveland, Ohio*).

So the Japanese navy believes it can fight America. That is the staggering part of the news. The navy had the last word; nobody could rush Japan into war without the navy's consent. The navy is a scientific service; its young officers are too busy to muddle their brains with pipe dreams. The navy has not lost its face in China. Before the Emperor gave the nod and grunt that okayed the order for Pearl Harbor, he must have said to the navy: "It's your responsibility; are you sure you can bring the Empire safely through it?" He would require an answer on "soul and conscience." He would say something like this: "I am responsible to the divine ancestors for the Empire they have placed in my hands. Are you prepared to answer to them for the fate of this Empire?" His mouthpiece would be old Admiral Suzuki, the Grand Chamberlain, who would not easily be fooled.

3

That order will destroy the Japanese navy. But the navy did not believe it was destroying itself. The admirals are different from the military gang—not as different as cheese from chalk, for they are all Japanese, but they are men of broad mind, broadly educated, and the generals are men of narrow mind, narrowly educated.

Before deciding to attack the United States the navy had first to convince itself that it could succeed. Then it had to communicate its confidence to the Emperor's advisers, every one of whom would be opposed to the plan. And probably is still opposed.

The navy believes it can defeat America. A delusion, yes, but not one reached in an emotional moment, not dictated by any consideration whatsoever except a cold calculation of chances. All the navy's natural bias went against fighting the two strongest naval powers. The army has never fought anybody except Chinese and it thinks it can lick the world. The navy has been brought up on Mahan and sea power. It was not surprised by Dunkirk, as the generals were. It knows that to a naval nation the sea is not a Maginot wall but an open road. "Very few people know the importance of sea power," Nomura said to me the day before he left for Washington, when we talked of Britain's chances against Germany. Nomura went to America as the navy's agent. He wanted to stop this war. So, at least, I believed after talking with him, and I think he was honest. Since coming here I have heard that he told the people in Washington that he had the navy's support. Of course; he would not have come otherwise. What is the Japanese navy's plan now? What has it got that we don't know?

[In a broadcast from New York a week later I put this idea more formally:

By the Japanese system of group dictatorship, the navy has the last word on the question of war with the United States, because it is the navy that has to fight that war. Before the Emperor and his advisers consented to yesterday's attack, the navy was undoubtedly asked in the most solemn and formal manner if it could carry through such a war successfully. If the navy had not possessed the confidence that this could be done, it would not have begun the offensive. Do not imagine that the Japanese allowed Hitler to inveigle them into a suicide pact, or to undertake a desperate adventure in order to assist his plans. In all such matters the Japanese are cautious opportunists, consulting their own interests alone.]

DECEMBER 8 (*Cleveland*).

How is Japan to be defeated? How long will it take?

Tonight a radio commentator told the air that the cocksure little Japs would soon be taught a lesson. But in the meantime . . . It reminded me of a story I heard in Tokyo from a Soviet Ambassador. At the very beginning of the Manchurian affair, when, as Mr. Stimson said, the Japanese army was running amuck, the Ambassador had talked to Mr. S. (a great Japanese industrialist; he is dead, but his family lives and his name had better remain unwritten). The Japanese predicted that the army would soon be brought under control. Like the old generals and the old statesmen, he thought the young officers were only suffering from a bad attack of suppressed chauvinism; he did not know that the age of military government had returned. "The day will come, and come soon," he said, "when a Japanese officer will not dare to show his face in the streets of Tokyo." "But in the meantime," said the Ambassador, with his malicious Slavic smile, "it is Mr. S. who is not seen on the streets."

The sinister element in the situation is its revelation of the mind of the Japanese navy. What the Japanese intend by this stab in the back is that their ships and plane carriers shall have the freedom of the Pacific for the first round of the war. What they are after is command of the air and the water—for a time—and they have convinced themselves that they can hold it long enough to allow Hitler to get in his blow somewhere else. The gangsters have always timed their blows, first the left and then the right. We shall hear from the Atlantic soon, but not until this blow has produced its calculated effect. Probably they expect a concentration of American effort in the Pacific and a consequent weakening in the Atlantic.

Some are saying that Hitler dragged Japan into this war. Nobody who knows the Japanese would say so. The Japanese would not lift a finger to save Hitler; their thoughts are for Japan first and only. Opportunism is their only principle. Their national motto is: "What the traffic will bear." That is the slogan they understand. Properly translated into classical ideographs, it would have a vogue like "Kodo"—the Imperial Way—meaning (to most of them): "Grab China while the grabbing is good," or "Kokuhan"—national emergency—meaning: "Now is the time the army should be boss."

They wrote the terms of the alliance in such a way that they are completely free to decide what they will do. The navy knows how little Hitler can do for Japan if and when the American and British battle fleets concentrate in the Pacific. In this round the Japanese navy is depending on itself *plus* what Hitler can do in the way of counter-irritant. The little Japanese admirals would not exaggerate that; they depend on themselves and what they have got under their hands.

Some of the newspapers are talking of national hara-kiri, as if the Naval General Staff were a young fool who had spent his boss's money in a geisha house. The *Cleveland Plain Dealer* repeats the fable that a responsible Japanese spokesman said: "Japan can't defeat China, nor can we accept a defeat from China. We can accept defeat from the United States and England. So let's have a quick war to save our face."

The bombing of the American ships as they lay in harbor was a nice beginning to a "gentlemanly" war, wasn't it? Does anyone suppose that the Japanese have forgotten what followed the sinking of the *Maine*? They know that Americans will not forget or forgive Pearl Harbor. They have never thought war was a game.

This is neither hara-kiri nor face-saving any more than it is Japan swinging into war in chivalrous obedience to an alliance that reads as if it had been drawn by a shyster lawyer.

I have heard nothing so loaded with unconscious ill-omen as those views. They show how little we know Japan. They won't last.

I told the conference [1] yesterday, just before the news came, that the chances of Japan's staying on the fence were rather better than fifty-fifty. I suggested fifty-one to forty-nine. This hope rested on the assumption that the navy, knowing America's ultimately overwhelming superiority of resources, would refuse to take it on.

Everything I had learned about the Japanese navy in twenty years supported the conservative view. There were many Nomuras in it. The army modeled itself on Germany's; its imitation was so slavish that it had introduced the custom of allowing non-coms to strike privates, and it compensated the privates by ordering foreigners in China to take off their hats when they passed a Japanese sentry, and allowing soldiers to beat

---

[1] A two-day conference organized by the Foreign Affairs Council of Cleveland, Ohio. It discussed the "merging wars"—Japan's war in China and Hitler's war in Europe. The *Cleveland Plain Dealer* reported:

"About 80 delegates from seven countries had gathered for an academic discussion of Far Eastern problems. For two days, the words had flowed without attempting to reach a conclusion. This was more of a mental exercise than a discussion of realities. Many of the experts had even predicted that there would be no war with Japan and gave good reasons to support their belief.

"The delegates spoke of 'the merging wars' in Europe and Asia. Then, suddenly, the wars merged. Edward C. Carter, secretary-general of the institute, broke into the program to announce that the Japanese had attacked Pearl Harbor.

"The delegates looked at each other with dazed expressions. A retired officer of the Indian Army held a silent head-to-head conference with a former manager of a Sumatra rubber plantation. Count Carlo Sforza, former Italian Foreign Minister, exchanged glances with a former German citizen. Four turbaned natives of India looked across the table at five U. S. congressmen who looked back at them. Chinese, Canadians, New Zealanders and Englishmen sat in stunned silence."

up anyone, man or woman, who did not show proper respect to the Imperial army. The navy had been only a little infected by the Nazism that had got into the army. I remembered that when the army mutinied in 1936 the government's first scared gesture was to send the fleet into Tokyo Bay. Seamen with bayonets, not soldiers, stood guard at the Navy Office and the houses of the admirals. The navy was the conservative element in the collective military dictatorship which governed Japan. Its traditions were formed on the British model, the army's on the German. Naval officers did not indulge in political speeches like the generals. The young naval officers made cruises to other countries. They knew something of the world beyond Japan.

The Japanese were thinking a great deal about their position at the peace conference. They wanted to keep the fleet intact so that they would have something in hand that would save them from being asked to wait on the mat, like Austria-Hungary after the last war. Japan's policy during the war of 1914–18 had been governed by the consideration that Japan could not afford to be on the losing side at any peace conference. It was this fear that had brought her into the war on the side of Britain and had caused subsequent shivering in the dark days when Germany seemed to be winning. "My poor country!" I heard a wealthy Japanese cry as he walked the porch of the country hotel where I was staying; "dragged into this war by a pro-British government."

What had occurred in 1941 to fetch the navy down from the fence where it had sat, turning a Nelsonian blind eye to the treaty Kurusu signed in Berlin?

The suicide suggestion is fantastic. Hara-kiri, the

belly-cut, has bemused the imagination of Westerns because we are saturated with Christian teaching. We think self-slaughter the irreparable and unforgivable sin. To the Japanese it is, at its best, the final evidence of "sincerity," and at its worst an unfortunate misdemeanor. Hara-kiri was the Japanese method of capital punishment for warriors and gentry. A nobleman who expiated a crime in that way did not suffer expropriation of his estates. It was a way of keeping the property in the family and escaping a more painful death. There was no gruesome disembowelment. The condemned person, in solemn surroundings, made a token cut with a dagger of which only a quarter-inch protruded from a white silk wrapping. His "friend" stood behind him with a two-handed sword, and at the moment the trickle of blood showed, he beheaded the prisoner with one stroke.

The Japanese as a race are not more addicted to suicide than many others. The fifteenth edition of the *Encyclopædia Britannica* places the suicide rate in Japan during the first quarter of the twentieth century rather below that of Germany and of most of the countries for which statistics are cited. It is true that Japanese sometimes commit suicide for what appear to us to be trivial reasons—business failure, embezzlement, fear of something they cannot bring themselves to face. A Japanese tennis player jumped off a steamer because he had yielded to pressure to play in an international contest and felt that he would fail. General Nogi committed hara-kiri after attending the funeral of his Emperor, but that was in 1912 and there has been no similar case. Three Japanese soldiers rushed a bomb into the Chinese wire at Shanghai and perished with it. Japan has never lacked soldiers and sailors who were ready to die. The feeling of responsibility to the Emperor and the country can be stronger than the love of life. But that feeling, perhaps the strongest of which the Japanese are capable, takes a different aspect when it is not the life of the individual but of the nation that is at stake. The Japanese can be fanatics individually, but as group thinkers they are cautious, calculating, and deliberate.

I do not know how many ships and planes the Japanese have, nor what use they plan to make of their "anchored aircraft carriers" in the Pacific, nor what stores they have of oil and gasoline and metals; but I know how they think, how they reach their decisions in such questions. The Naval General Staff in Tokyo is no battle-drunk group with romantic ideas of a glorious doom; it is not inspired by any concern for Germany's fate. It seeks one thing only: success for Japan; and it would not act until it had convinced itself that it had much more than a fifty-fifty chance of success. That conviction was reached on a careful and conservative estimation of the factors and resources available. Japanese resources are greater and their plans bolder than we know. The China war has been a training ground for naval fliers. The army may be bogged down, but the navy has had four years on a war footing and unlimited budgets, all spent in preparation for the struggle now on.

It was consciously a bold decision, and it will in the end prove suicidal, but the Japanese Naval General Staff looked to the end before they made the beginning. They did not move before they had convinced themselves that they could win.

DECEMBER 9 (*New York*).

People here are wild at the insolence of the "little Japs," whom they thought of as comic figures. They don't yet realize how calculated was that insolence.

It follows as the day the night that the Japanese navy is satisfied that it has the ships, planes, and supplies needed for the greatest struggle in its history. That struggle, on all the visible evidence, is doomed to ultimate failure unless . . .

Unless the attack on Pearl Harbor has crippled the American sea and air forces there for the period estimated in the Japanese time-table. In that period the Germans, fully informed of the Japanese plans and in contact with their agents over here, will strike their blow.

The Germans cannot reach the Pacific. Where, then? An all-out effort to invade England?

A project they couldn't or wouldn't carry out when the British army was disorganized and had lost its equipment and when British defenses were unready does not seem hopeful now when the army has been re-equipped and reinforced, and when the home defenses are organized and the food supply replenished.

Will Hitler renew the Battle of the Atlantic on a bigger scale, reverting to the purpose of defeating England with the weapon he believes defeated Germany in 1918—starvation through blockade? If so, the Japanese are reckoning on a public clamor in the United States ("Remember the *Maine*") which will force the President to draw ships and planes from the Atlantic to the Pacific.

Against that is the fact that submarine action in the North Atlantic in winter is difficult and has been made more hazardous by stronger defenses. But if the American fleet is weakened in the Atlantic, will the balance of chances swing over to the Axis side?

Can England be defeated in the Battle of the Atlantic?

Will Hitler take Spain and Portugal for airfields which would enable his planes to range out over the Atlantic and intensify the starvation strategy?

Does the plan include getting hold of the French fleet, seizing Dakar, and stirring up trouble in South America, again designed to divide American and British action, lessen the pressure on Japan in the Pacific, and reduce the forces operating on the Iceland life line?

How about the time factor? French navy crews could not be depended on. German crews could be supplied without difficulty and may be ready now in occupied France. But they would need time to become acquainted with the French ships. And the British might repeat Oran. Any or all of these plans might be accompanied by another winter of night bombing intended to "soften" the British people.

I don't think such plans would arouse much enthusiasm in the Navy Office in Tokyo. . . . Heavens, I see it again as I type the words. The old Jack Tar doorkeepers who asked your number and grinned and bowed when I told them mine was Number One; the cool square lobby on the first floor with its obsolete quick-firer kept on show for some reason I never troubled to ask; that hole under the stairs where I had so many talks with Admiral X, as jovial a seaman as I have ever known. He never told me anything, but I liked talking to him. . . .

Where so much is hidden, let us start from points we can take to be true.

First, the Japanese navy did not get into this until it believed it had secured itself and the Empire against defeat.

Second, the Japanese are not in it to help Hitler, but to help themselves.

Japanese strategy has not changed in forty years. They began the Russian war with a torpedo attack on the Russian fleet as it lay in port forty-eight hours before they declared war. They began this war in Honolulu on a Sunday while their envoys were talking in the State Department at Washington.

That also was true to Japanese form. On the very night the Japanese torpedo-boats crept into Port Arthur, the Japanese minister at St. Petersburg was attending a ball in the Imperial Palace. He went there feeling very uneasy lest his host and hostess might have heard the news. But the Russians did not know what had happened in far-away Port Arthur until next day, and the Japanese diplomat basked in the smiles of the Czar and the Czarina and went home and smugly recorded in his diary how he had fooled the Russians. I wonder if Kurusu keeps a diary.

In 1904 the Japanese wanted to knock out the Russian Far Eastern fleet while they moved their transports over to Manchuria. On Sunday they tried to knock out American sea and air power before they landed armies in Malaya and Luzon.

Sunday's raids were the first swift, deadly flash to stun the enemy. The body blows will come next. Singapore is one objective; American air and sea power is the other.

To know why the Japanese are attacking Singapore, ask what they need. They need the oil, rubber, and tin of the Dutch East Indies and Malaya. America has plenty of oil, but it needs rubber and tin, and Japan wants to be able to refuse those munitions materials to the United States. Japanese invaders cannot get at the Dutch East Indies as long as Singapore functions. Singapore stands at the crossroads of the South Seas. It is like a traffic policeman; the gangsters cannot get into the bank round the corner until the cop is out of the way. The Philippines must also be attacked because planes from the islands can maul the Japanese troopships. Japan must have air supremacy over the Philippines.

Admit that Japan wins the first round by its special tactics. The real struggle comes afterwards. Ultimately superior power, resources, brains, will tell.

"Wars are not won by machinery alone, but by the human spirit." That thought came across the air last night. I subscribe to it with all my heart, but machinery is also useful. "God (which is a way of saying the human spirit) fights on the side of the big battalions." The big battalions in this war are against Japan as well as is the spirit of America. The Japanese admirals understand the former though not the latter.

There is a curious resemblance between the German and the Japanese problems. England cannot easily get at Hitler, but Hitler, by his occupation of French, Belgian, Dutch and Norwegian bases, can get at England. Japan cannot easily get at the home territory of the United States, and will make no serious attempt, though raids will be organized to alarm the Pacific states and detain for their defense ships and planes which would be better used in hitting at Japanese power in the Orient.

Nor can America easily get at Japan's home territory; both general staffs are fighting with the knowledge that the blows fall far from the heart. But Japan can easily reach the United States' Far Eastern outposts, and when and if she has occupied, or contained, the strategic points, Japan will expect to keep her own forces beyond the reach of anything but the greatest and most difficult efforts. The war cannot be carried to the cities of Japan unless Russia comes in.

With American air power temporarily weakened, American bases occupied, Singapore captured or muzzled, and with the Dutch East Indies in their hands, the Japanese are calculating that they can fight a defensive war for an indefinite time. They might capture Rangoon, cutting the Burma Road at its base.

A thought has come that looks crazy but it won't go away. I'll put it down. It won't be the first time paradox has been true in Japan. We think the Japanese do things backwards, but it all depends on the point of view.

The Japanese may be preparing for a German defeat.

Reasons? They know what to expect if the Axis is smashed and they are still extended in China. They know the conditions they will face then. The United States will have a navy and air force of unprecedented

size; the British navy will be at the top of its form; in
science as well as numbers both forces will have out-
stripped Japan, for the Japanese always lag behind the
results of research in better-equipped countries. The
combined fleets of the victorious democracies will appear in the seas and skies of the East, and Japan will be
summoned to evacuate China. If she refuses, the democracies can pour their huge surplus of tanks,
guns, and equipment into that country and can lend
Chiang Kai-shek military advisers who know how to
use them. They can hunt the Japanese fleet into its
hiding-places and keep it there while Japan is blockaded. They will deprive Japan of her war loot, past and
present—Manchuria, Formosa, the mandated islands,
perhaps even Korea. This was the prospect the Japanese had to prepare against. From that point of view
their move is intelligible.

Some remarkable calculations have been made in
Berlin and Tokyo. How much air power does Japan
need to enable her to take Singapore, seize or destroy
the American bases in the Philippines, and grab the
Dutch East Indies? Just how difficult is it going to be
for the United States to reinforce its air power in the
Far East after the stepping-stones and refueling stations—Guam, Wake, and Midway—are lost? If Japan
gets the Dutch bases, how many planes will she be able
to send back home for defense against American attacks from Siberia or Dutch Harbor? As to Dutch Harbor, how much assistance do the Japanese expect from
the worst weather in the world—perpetual gales in winter, fog in summer?

We are not yet accustomed to the conception of

global war. We think of separate theaters, the Atlantic, the Middle East, Russia, the Far East. But our enemies are thinking in terms of global war. A spring attack on Egypt would be global strategy. If Germany got Suez while Japan got Singapore, the two ends of the Axis would meet in the Indian Ocean. Oil, rubber, tin, sugar, and rice would flow to hungry Germany, and German weapons would be shipped to Japan. Half the world would be theirs; they would expect to sit on their gains and tell us our day was done. And even if the German end of such a plan failed, the Japanese might be masters of everything between Honolulu and the Bay of Bengal.

Conclusion: the Japanese have made their plans for a long war, and they have not left out the possibility of a German defeat.

If this analysis is anywhere near accurate, the Japanese plan is a long-range one. The Japanese believe that the treacherous assault of December 7, followed up by what Hitler will do to divide America's strength, will give them the mastery of the air and the sea in the western Pacific long enough to let them carry out their program. They expect to deprive America of all its existing bases nearer than Hawaii. They expect to capture or surround Singapore and make the waters around it too hot for British warships. They expect to defeat the defenders of the Philippines and then transfer their forces to the Dutch East Indies. They can then "dig in" behind their screen of islands and the huge spaces of the Pacific, reckoning that the time and effort needed to dislodge them will be so great that even a victorious America will hesitate.

Perhaps there will be another peace offer; the Japanese share Hitler's delusion that people would sooner make peace with him than die fighting him—but there is too much wishful thinking about such speculations. It would be a legitimate inference, however, that behind this strategy is an "either-or" dilemma—either the democracies must face the prospect of another war, with their enemies holding positions from which it will be hard to dislodge them, or they must agree to peace terms which will leave the Japanese New Order in being.

It is worse than useless to think that superior resources will bring us victory on a silver platter. Those resources are latent; war is dynamic. There must be an unwavering will to "fight it out on this line" if it takes not all summer, but ten years. Japan has become a "national defense state" in which all the energies of the nation are harnessed to war, and everything above bare subsistence is devoted to aggression. We also must convert ourselves into a "national defense state" in which all that we have is thrown into the struggle. Only thus can we preserve and hand down to the future the most humane way of life the world has known.

CHAPTER II

THE JAPANESE MIND AND PLAN

THE mind of the Japanese navy is the mind that will fight this war and that we will fight. What sort of mind is it?

The average Japanese naval officer one met in Tokyo was a likable human being. Unlike his military confreres, he was easy in foreign company and no problem to his hostess. The navy's original British training still marked his style; he "came out to meet you"; there was no clicking of heels and mimicry of the very high and puissant Prussian staff officer. In leisure hours he was "clubbable." Diplomatic ladies liked Japanese naval officers and found them light in hand. They were frank in all that was unimportant. All this is merely saying that the sea sets the same stamp on a man the world over. Those personal qualities gained for the Japanese navy a reputation for common sense and broad views (as compared with the army) which has not stood the acid test.

When we examine the Japanese naval mind in action and in policy we can see that in a recent space of time— less than ten years—it has followed the same track as the army's. The corruption of the Japanese army is a long story and it is complicated by the fact that the natural and cultivated nationalism of the Japanese soldier has been subjected to the influence of Marxism. The Japanese officer, who was always a chauvinist, is now a Nazi. The corruption of the army broke into the open in 1931 and it had then gone too far to be checked.

The change in the navy was not apparent until 1935. It began to germinate slowly after the Washington Conference in 1922. By the peace treaties Japan had been given the German islands in the Pacific. Marxist ideas working upon a native love of war produced the military socialism which today rules Japan. Acquisition of three great fleets of "anchored aircraft carriers" in the Pacific working on naval minds angered by the inferior Washington ratio eventually produced the plan which burst out like a volcano on December 7.

Japan's naval policy before then had been rational and above-board. It was based on essential needs and on a policy which did not anticipate war with England or the United States, and never dreamed of fighting America and England together, with China and perhaps Russia thrown in. Japan complains that she is encircled; never did any nation so deliberately encircle itself with powers which only wanted to be let alone. Japanese will question the rightness of the word "deliberately." Those who opposed the war and fear its results would substitute "blunderingly." We may agree that choosing a demonstrably wrong policy and sticking to it no matter where it leads is deliberate blundering.

The Japanese navy's primary function as it was conceived until 1935 was to maintain command of the near seas where the shipping lanes converge and which give Japan access to the mainland of Asia. This was perfectly legitimate and was publicly recognized in the decisions of the Washington Conference. A secondary function, not formally recognized but so closely connected with the first that a fleet that could fulfill one could also fulfill the other, was to furnish a screen of naval power strong enough to prevent foreign interference with Japan's policies in China. Both were conceded in the Washington agreements. China policy was embodied in the Nine-Power Treaty and it was not then realized by the statesmen who signed it that Japanese "sincerity" required a treaty to be ignored when one of the parties had grown dissatisfied with it. The Washington naval agreements stabilized the fleets of Japan, the United States, and Britain in such proportions that Japan was left in undisputed mastery of the near seas. Pearl Harbor, 3,380 nautical miles from Japan, and Singapore, 3,345 miles, were the sentry-boxes marking the limits of Japan's naval domain. The condition was that peace was to be maintained and the rights of Japan's weaker neighbors respected. But the Japanese army and navy had never thought that condition material. Their duty, as they read it, was to make Japan great, and the means was their possession of armaments stronger than those of all the other Asiatic nations combined.

The acquisition of the mandated islands and a study of their strategic possibilities in the air age changed the original defensive policy into one which looked far beyond the protection of Japan's principal sea routes and the promotion of her policy in China. The islands provided a Maginot wall built by coral insects, behind which lay the wealth of the Dutch East Indies. The South Sea policy began to look practicable. Organizations with official backing sprang up to promote it. The governors of Formosa were thenceforth selected from among the senior admirals. Foreigners were prevented from visiting the Bonin Islands; an Anglican Bishop making his yearly visit to the small congregation there was shadowed by Japanese policemen and forbidden to return. A Japanese lady born in Bonin who lived near me in Tokyo found herself under surveillance every summer when her relatives from the island paid their yearly visit.

The naval treaties expired in 1935. Before they were abrogated the Japanese navy was at work on the islands and it has been at work on them ever since. The screen which the Japanese were able to erect around China was extended to surround the regions whence the world draws most of its rubber and tin.

The destruction of the naval-limitation agreements caused some disquiet in Japan. A few far-seeing men, accustomed to look beneath the surface, were asking if the Japanese navy expected war with America. They did not use their influence to have the issue raised in the legislature or in any public way. The era of government by assassination had begun and neither capitalists nor politicians cared to expose themselves to the fate of Prime Minister Inukai, Finance Minister Inouye, and financial magnate Baron Dan.

The navy nevertheless started a campaign of reassurance. The public was told that America's plans were known and that means existed by which American naval superiority could be reduced to less than parity. Even parity, it was held, could not endanger Japan, because of her geographical advantages. The American fleet, it was said, had devised a "ring formation" which would be used to bring the Japanese fleet to battle or force it to take shelter in its home bases. According to those accounts, the American battle fleet, surrounded by a huge screen of submarines, destroyers, and cruisers and escorted by aircraft carriers, was to advance across the Pacific from Pearl Harbor. That fleet was superior to the Japanese fleet in the ratio of 10 to 6 capital ships, but . . .

Japanese annual reports to the League of Nations on her Pacific mandate were punctually rendered, even after Japan had left the League. They regularly reported that no fortifications were being constructed on the islands. None were necessary, in the strict sense of the term. All that the Japanese navy needed was anchorages for commercial shipping and fueling stations for commercial aircraft. The Japanese people were told that Japan was able by her anchored aircraft carriers, supported by ocean-going submarines, to make an American fleet movement into the western Pacific too hazardous to attempt.

The American navy had an alternative route, via Australia and Singapore, but that route by reason of distance and absence of bases was considered second-rate. The northern route to Japan, via Dutch Harbor, was dismissed as impracticable because of distance, fogs, gales, and Japan's powerful home bases.

Acquisition of the mandated islands fundamentally altered and enlarged Japan's naval strategy. Until their possibilities had been analyzed, Japan's naval policy was co-operation. The change to absolute non-co-operation was the sign that a new naval policy had been born. In the China war the policy was developed. Hainan island was seized in violation of a Japanese treaty with France, and the naval governor of Formosa announced that henceforth he would administer the Spratley Reefs. The Spratley Reefs, an ownerless group lying off the main traffic routes through the South China Sea, are one of the least known regions of the globe. They consist of ninety-six islets, the surfaces of which are barely above sea level. Shipmasters passing down the China Sea give that treacherous waste of coral a wide berth, but the Japanese navy has surveyed and sounded it and Japanese ships can pass freely through the reefs and shelter in the lagoons. The armada that invaded the Philippines may have assembled there.

The evolution of Japanese policy can be read on the map. Her home islands lie off the western end of Asia like a fortified breakwater a thousand miles long. By taking Formosa from China, Japan extended that fortified breakwater and got a jumping-off place for South China and the Philippines. Her naval station in the Pescadores, off the Formosan coast, was the first base for Japanese air raids into China; it is one of the bases from which Japanese bombers set out for Manila. The seizure of Hainan and the annexation of the Spratley Reefs have been told. Then came the occupation of Indo-China, by arrangement with the defeatists of Vichy, and the invasion of Thailand when the first attempts at bribery with French territory had failed. By these means the Japanese navy assured itself of sheltered bases from which it can operate at great distances from its home ports and prepared itself for the Pacific war it is now fighting.

From the preparations the Japanese navy has made we can know its plan. It expects to have attained possession of the South Seas before the struggle with Hitler is over. Once in, it believes it cannot be dislodged without a new war in which Japan will have many advantages she now lacks.

How can that plan be defeated?

Questions of strategy and tactics must be left to the general staffs. They cannot be answered in advance, for this is a new war. It is air war at its highest power —"the nations' airy navies grappling in the central blue" —on a more gigantic scale than we have ever known. New strategies, new tactics will be worked out as the war goes on. The types of aircraft with which we began the war will be antiquated when we end it. Tactics will be evolved for machines that count their mileage in seconds. Strategy will work among calculations of immense distances annihilated by speed, yet with all its operations conditioned by the need of fuel. An army marches on its belly; the plane is chained to a gasoline tank.

Capture of the Philippines, Singapore, and the Dutch East Indies is essential to the Japanese plan. Japan then expects to have the advantage of the inner position in her war with the United States and Britain, as Germany has had in all her wars.

It will be something new in inner positions. Starting from about the same latitude as Montreal, it sweeps 3,700 miles south, rests on those fleets of "anchored aircraft carriers" at the equator, turns west by south among a continent of coral islands of which the neo-English cities of Australia, "down under," have suddenly become conscious, and goes north again by Singapore. The Malay Peninsula, jutting out from the center of Asia, is another gigantic breakwater fencing its western wall. It is big enough to hold the American continent from Port Churchill on Hudson Bay to Quito on the equator, with the West Indies thrown in. This area Japan has elected to conquer and then defend. It is as if Asia, the teeming continent, were presenting an embattled front to the world. Only it is not Asia; it is a pugnacious tribe trying to dominate Asia and holding down enemies within while fighting enemies without.

Possession of this area carries advantages and risks, and both, like itself, are gigantic. It gives Japan the supplies, notably oil, she has long coveted. She doubtless expects the Dutch wells to be destroyed and believes that her engineers can quickly get them going again. It gives her enemies a truly formidable task if they are to dig her out. But Japanese success requires two conditions: those supplies must be sufficient for the vastest kind of war ever undertaken, and they must be universal in nature. If one essential element is lacking, Japan has a heel of Achilles which a war of attrition will surely find out.

Japan still has 600,000 or 800,000 troops dispersed over thousands of miles in China and another 300,000 stationed along the Manchurian border to guard against

CHAPTER III

IMMENSITIES

THE war that the Japanese have brought on is war in the air in its biggest form. Before it ends, the pace and the range will be something never seen before. The Tokyo strategists saw that it would be air war with ocean bases; they could not foresee—and we cannot—the dimensions and the acceleration it will attain.

The game will be played in the vastest arena the world has ever known. Compared with the European theaters of battle, the Pacific is as the Yankee Stadium to a village diamond. You can sail the Pacific for weeks without seeing anything above the water except your own ship and the flying fishes. The battle area is planetary in its dimensions. Here are a few of the distances marking the approximate limits of the field in statute miles (figures supplied by the *New York Times*):

San Francisco to Pearl Harbor	2,402 miles
Pearl Harbor to Sydney	5,063 "

Sydney to Port Darwin	{ by boat,	2,820 miles
	{ by air,	1,950 "
Port Darwin to Singapore		2,450 "
Singapore to Manila		1,576 "
Manila to Yokohama		2,033 "
Japan to Dutch Harbor		2,933 "

The distances within this area which the air forces will have to traverse are commensurately Gargantuan:

Manila to Guam	1,589 miles
Guam to Wake	1,508 "
Wake to Midway	1,185 "
Midway to Honolulu	1,304 "

Even from Australia there are big leaps:

Port Darwin to Timor	375 miles
Timor to Singapore	by air, 1,650 "

If any Philippine bases are held and can be reinforced they will make things difficult for the Japanese outposts. The distances are:

Manila to Formosa	by air, 530 miles
Manila to Hainan	" " 775 "

Every mile means gasoline, and gasoline means filling stations. We can get plenty of gasoline, but the widow's cruse that automatically refills itself has not been rediscovered. The filling stations in this war are islands and the Japanese have 2,400 of these spreading from their mainland 2,000 miles southward towards the Dutch East Indies and Australia and 2,000 miles eastward towards Hawaii. The problem is not how to fight the Japanese planes but how to get the American planes to the ring. It is a problem that will give a headache to the experts, and armchair experts may save their aspirin.

In this kind of war the Japanese will encounter a wave of the future. They will meet American inventiveness, American technical skill, American design, and American industry. These are the decisive factors, though at the moment we cannot measure them or deploy them at full strength among the islands of the Pacific. Their present power is enormously greater than Japan's and their potential, as compared with Japan's, is for practical purposes illimitable. These are the foes Japan has challenged.

If the position Japan intends to take up compels America to move great distances, it also compels Japan to defend immense lines. It will not be necessary to dig the Japanese out of every islet. With Hitler defeated, the blockade will be completely closed and the western Pacific will become a prison yard. The stoppage of supplies will be absolute except for those Japan can develop in the conquered areas. We shall see distances annihilated that now seem insurmountable. British and Australian islands flank the Japanese sphere. Port Darwin will become a base of American air operations. Bases will be found; it is physically impossible for Japan to control thousands upon thousands of islands. The Japanese will be raided at many points, and they will have to maintain an alert along immense distances. Lengthening lines of communication, the bugbear of every commander, will present a succession of problems to minds from which spontaneity has been educated out. The pace will be made too hot for Japan to sustain. She will find, as she found in China, that though she has won territory she cannot exploit its resources as fast as war eats them up.

When Hitler is out of the way, China can be munitioned on a scale Japan's arsenals cannot match. Tanks, planes, guns of all kinds will flow in over the railways that are now being built to replace and supplement the Burma Road. And Russia, Japan's implacable enemy, waits grimly at the northern gate. Operations from Russian airfields, and these alone, can devastate the Japanese cities; if and when American bombers and fighters get bases in Siberia, Japan's great cities will become untenable. Sporadic raids can doubtless be endured—unlike California, Japan has been practicing black-outs for six or seven years—but not the continuous destruction that American planes, set free from the war against Hitler, can inflict.

Until Hitler attacked Russia, Japanese militarists could obtain German technical assistance and some valuable though not bulky German war material by the Trans-Siberian Railway. That road is closed and except for an occasional and very uncertain blockade-runner which may succeed in rounding the Horn or the Cape of Good Hope, German technical assistance must be limited to information sent by wireless. It is not probable that the Germans will confide their best secrets to the air when so many spies are listening in. German science is blockaded as well as German gunsights.

Japan's reserve supplies of military materials and fuels are larger than anyone suspected. The facts are probably known to less than twenty men in Japan, most of whom could be named—the chiefs of the Naval and Military General Staffs, the Ministers of War and the

Navy, the Inspector General of Military Aviation and his opposite number in the high places of the navy, the Inspector General of Military Training, and the confidential aides and experts of those executives; certainly to the Emperor and probably to Mr. Seihin Ikeda, the former executive head of the great Mitsui corporation, who is now attached to the Emperor as one of his personal consultants. The Japanese veneration for "military secrets" is such that it is unlikely that any civilians know the details. The military chiefs alone know where those reserves are stored and they alone know the exact quantity and quality.

Estimates have been published and can be disregarded. Example: it was asserted that Japan's reserves of oil are 60,000,000 barrels and her annual consumption 35,000,000 barrels. The demands of a great war, utterly unlike the China war, would double the consumption and inside a year at most the Japanese war machine would come to a standstill like a car whose driver had forgotten to call at the filling station. But the Japanese have made their calculations on the basis of actual figures, not estimates. We can see from their actions that they are satisfied that they have enough fuel to take them where they mean to go. I do not know what oil and gasoline their well-concealed tanks in Japan may hold, but I am certain the Naval General Staff did not go to war with the United States on a short supply.

CHAPTER IV

WHO RUNS JAPAN?

THE question is purely pragmatical. We have to know
the people we are fighting though we did not want to
fight them and took pains to avoid provoking them. We
are not seeking political or legal answers—and, anyhow,
the Japanese system is still half-baked and unfinished
and it conforms to no familiar political pattern—but we
must know how it works. We want to know how policies are incubated in Japan, how decisions are taken,
and who takes them. We want to know what internal
trouble-making factors a Japanese government has to
reckon with in conducting its affairs with us. We want
to know if the circumstances of the Japanese nation
force its government into any particular line of policy.
How much or how little weight should we give to the
argument that, in the last analysis, economic necessity
caused this war?

Merely to read the news about Japan it is necessary

to have some idea of the kind of political machinery the Japanese work with. During the fifteen months when Japan hovered on the brink but shrank from the plunge into war, the news reports from Japan contained many delayed predictions. How often were we told—usually from sources outside of Japan—that Japan was about to seize the Netherlands East Indies, to invade Siberia, or to present an ultimatum to Siam. Japan has now done several of these things and may do them all; that powerful elements in Japan wanted to do them was always obvious; there was a perpetual agitation for something to be done, perpetual talk about doing it, and yet for over a year after the alliance with Germany was signed it did not get done. Somewhere in Japan there was reluctance to "go the whole hog" and fight the United States.

The difference or the delay between prediction and event was due in the first place to the manner in which the Japanese reach their major decisions. Fence-sitting meant that in the inner circles of government those who had a say in the final decision were not yet satisfied and therefore the step which seemed imminent was not taken. The Prime Minister or the War Minister who seemed to be leading the activists was in fact often engaged in restraining them, and even when he gave way, like Konoye, who made the alliance with Germany when the army finally insisted on it, there was sometimes a mental reservation which prevented the action from having its full consequences immediately.

It would help clear thinking if words like "dictatorship," "democracy," "Fascism," "liberalism" could be left out of discussions on Japanese politics. Unfortunately they cannot; they are the current coin of modern political talk; the Japanese themselves use them just as they use such phrases as "the Japanese Monroe Doctrine" to describe something quite different from the Monroe Doctrine. All such terms have a different scale of values from ours. General Senjuro Hayashi, when he became Prime Minister for a few months, was fond of announcing his devotion to constitutional politics, but he was careful to add "constitutional politics peculiar to Japan." By "constitutional politics peculiar to Japan," Japan has become a Nazi-Fascist state without a Nazi or Fascist party. It was possible to do this within the framework of the constitution. Japan has not lost a "liberal" system under the assaults of a Nazi-minded army; she never had such a system. Government in Japan today is virtually a dictatorship, but it is dictatorship with a difference; it is not exercised by a dictator with a supposedly national party behind him and a blare of propaganda going before him. For Germany you can say Hitler; for Russia Stalin, and for Italy Mussolini. No name leaps up for Japan, and it is not because Japanese names are queer but because in Japan no individual leader holds such authority.

Japanese politics and government must be seen as part of Japanese psychology. The Japanese conception of government has grown from the family system. By the conception or idea of government I mean simple fundamental principles. The plainest American citizen, working with his hands in field or factory, might not be able to express the idea of American government in scientific language, but he knows that his government is founded on majority rule. The idea is government by the people.

He knows what a vote is. But majority rule, simple and conclusive as it appears to us, seems to the Japanese a complex and unsatisfactory basis. During the last World War an American Ambassador took pains to explain to a friendly group of young Japanese the principles of democracy. Early in the proceedings he struck a snag. He had been appointed by President Wilson, and President Wilson, in his first term, was a minority President. Even admitting the majority principle, said the Japanese, how can you ask the nation to be loyal to a chief who did not have a majority?

The family system is the foundation of Japanese society; it is and has been for centuries a legal and social institution of vital importance in Japanese life. Japan is not a nation of individuals but of families. The Japanese mind is saturated with the family system. Every great decision in a Japanese person's life—education, career, marriage—is the result of a family council's judgment.

It is difficult to suggest a comparison which will not mislead more than it will enlighten. You might say that with us it is a fundamental concept that if an adult individual makes up his or her mind to a certain course in his lawful affairs, no one has the right to prevent him. With the Japanese an opposite concept prevails. The individual has not got the moral right to do anything without the approval of his family, if it is a family affair, or in wider matters, of all his associates who are interested.

To see how this inherited mental background affects politics, compare a family council with a town meeting. What is wanted in each case is a decision, but it will be sought in different ways. The town meeting will proceed by a majority vote; the family council will not act, generally speaking, while there is an absence of agreement among its principal members.

We hear plenty about the delays of democracy due to the long process needed to make up the many-millioned mind. But the Japanese also suffer from delays. They missed the first—and perhaps the last—bus for their South Sea policy in the summer of 1940 when, after Dunkirk, they failed to attack Singapore and secure the key to the Dutch East Indies and the western Pacific.

The most important political fact about Japan today is that it has not finished the revolution that began in 1868. That revolution destroyed feudalism, but it did not set up a strong central government in its place. It restored the Emperor. But the Emperor had not been an executive ruler for centuries; he did not even live at the seat of government. In restoring the Emperor, a youth of sixteen, the victorious clans were not restoring an autocrat or even a Charles II ready and able to govern. They were installing themselves in the place of the previous clan government. They continued to use the methods of government the country was accustomed to. The broader system they set up admitted the new groups which arose in a modernized society and established a central administration in place of the three hundred odd clans, but it did not find and has not yet found a strong central authority capable of controlling all groups; the government of Japan was and is today a shifting balance of groups. A Japanese statesman once illustrated the system by taking a handful of pencils from his desk. He arranged them roughly in the form of a pyramid supported by his hand and showed how the pressure of his fingers changed the direction in which the pyramid pointed. "That is the Japanese government," he said; "sometimes its policy aims in one direction and sometimes in another; it all depends on the pressure at the base."

The groups are always changing. Twenty years ago the most powerful group was the Genro, or "Elder Statesmen." They were able to control both the army and the bureaucrats and they exercised something very like supreme power. The Elder Statesmen were in their day all-powerful and they seemed indispensable, yet the institution is now extinct.

Another group, consisting of the legislature and the political parties, was of high importance once; it seemed to be the rising force of new Japan. But now not only party government but the parties themselves are things of the past.

Are they dead, or have they been blackjacked into inanition? Personally, and admitting that it may be wishful thinking, I believe that on the day of defeat they will begin to recover vitality, though no doubt the resurrection will take place in a Japanese body.

Books, reports, and magazine articles, including my own, written on the development of representative government in Japan have turned out to be for the most part waste paper. The reason is that the two houses, the ballot boxes, quadrennial elections, manhood suffrage, and debates in the house were, so to speak, imported novelty goods, got because they looked well, because the public wanted them, because other people had them, because Japan needed a new modern system of government to replace feudalism and naturally copied methods she saw working out well elsewhere. Nations can only use the political tools they understand. Parliament was only a group; it was never conceived of as the final essence of all groups. When a stronger group clashed with it, parliament went down. Its pretensions were reduced to impotence by the superior power of the army as the throne some centuries earlier had been reduced to impotence by the military clans.

There is a temptation to digress here into a very wide field. It could be pointed out that in the present resurgence of military government Japan is running true to historical form. Once before in her history Japan imported new institutions from abroad but the reformed civilian government was succeeded by a military rule which, if we may judge from its duration, nearly a thousand years, seemed to suit her. From the beginning of her history the dominant power in Japan has been the military. It would be easy to demonstrate that until the power and prestige of the Japanese army is broken, Japan will remain an aggressive country, a menace to her weaker neighbors and a nuisance to those who are stronger. But Japanese history is paradoxical and the conclusion that the Japanese are incurably militaristic over-simplifies its lesson. How do we explain why an aggressive people with a military government had until fifty years ago no record of foreign conquest? Japanese history also demonstrates that the Japanese are a most unadventurous people. They have no Genghis Khan, no Christopher Columbus. They locked themselves in their islands and developed a way of life which concerned itself with little things and made them things of beauty and was extraordinarily charming. With a record which embraces such contradictions it is wisest to refrain from positive conclusions and confine ourselves to asking what is at this moment the government of Japan with which our own government is at war.

The executive elements of the Japanese government which between them decide its policy are the Throne, the Cabinet, and the fighting services, and the last two are the predominant partners.

Language exhausts itself when the Japanese talk of their Emperor. He is divine; he is directly descended from the Sun Goddess. He is the sole center of unity in the Japanese nation; in him all power subsists. But such ideas are mystical, not political. The Japanese cannot translate them into political language. The Emperor, whose power is supposed to transcend that of all his subjects, can act as a ruler only on the advice of his responsible advisers. His chief official civilian adviser and executant is the Prime Minister, yet though the Emperor appoints the Prime Minister he does not choose him; the Prime Minister is recommended to the ruler by a group which has no authority for the action other than custom. The army and navy chiefs exercise another part of the Imperial power and do so independently of the Prime Minister. He is nominally the head of the Japanese government, but he cannot interfere with anything pertaining to defense. The system is obviously defective, but the Japanese can only use the instruments they have, and their great difficulty is that they have not agreed among themselves where the center of power rests. The Emperor does not exercise power as the Russian czars did; he is the reservoir from which power flows. Two of its major outlets have been permanently entrusted to the military and naval chiefs though they individually are but temporary spigots. The other major outlet is held for irregular periods by Prime Ministers, who have often in the last ten years been chosen almost by chance because they were supposed to be able to control the army or the navy. Like that curious official, the Eletto, whom the Spanish soldiers elected when they mutinied, the Japanese Emperor is clothed with supreme power but forbidden to use it. He does not govern. He is a dictator who cannot dictate but can only register the decrees of others.

The Emperor's "divinity" has always been a stumbling-block to Americans. The difficulty is due to the different scale of values. The Japanese peasant, soldier, artisan, or teacher does not imagine that the Emperor is endowed with supernatural power, nor do they pray to him as the Catholic prays to the Virgin or the saints. They know that he is a man like other men—he used to be provided with twelve concubines—and that he will one day die. The cult of Emperor-worship in Japan, however, is more to the Japanese than the worship of Augustus was to the Romans. The Romans were expressing in the manner of their age the greatest admiration one man can entertain for another; they were proclaiming that they held Cæsar in reverence like a god. In Japan religion has not drawn a clear line between the human and the divine. The woods and mountains are still the home of local deities. The family shrine in every household is a perpetual reminder that the ancestors and progenitors of the family have become "gods." The Imperial line was founded by the gods of Japan, and their divinity dwells in it, but the gods of Japan are never conceived of as the eternal spirit who made and rules the universe and will one day judge all men. They are to the nation and the race what those local deities of wood and stream are to the locality in which they dwell. They are the spirit of the race, and the living Emperor is its incarnation and symbol. He is not a leader as Cæsar was. The Emperor of Japan can dispense with the childish fiction which depicts Corporal Hitler poring over maps with his field marshals. He is the supreme source of power, yet he does not rule; he is responsible to the divine ancestors for the acts of his reign, and responsibility lies heavy on him today, yet he is not responsible for the acts of his ministers. He is assisted and advised by men who are placed in positions where they have the responsibility of assisting and advising him, yet he does not select those servants who hold such a grave responsibility; they are selected by those whose duty it is to select them. Everywhere is delegation and distribution of responsibility. If the Japanese system has any central principle it is the principle of figurehead government.

By the Throne is meant the Emperor and what may be called, for want of a more definite name, the Court. It is not a party; it is a few high and very carefully chosen officials who are bound together only by their common responsibility for assisting and advising the Emperor in the exercise of his political duties. It constitutes a definite group, the members of which are appointed by the Prime Minister of the day but are thereafter independent and irremovable except by the Emperor. This group of the Emperor's most intimate advisers consists of four officials: the Lord Keeper of the Imperial Seals, the Minister of the Imperial Household, the Grand Chamberlain, and the Grand Master of Ceremonies. The most important is the Lord Keeper. The office has acquired its importance partly because it was held for a number of years by an extremely able man, but essentially because it is necessary that the Japanese Emperor should have beside him faithful and independent advisers of high caliber if he is not to become again a nonentity as his ancestors were for a thousand years while the soldiers ruled the country. The Emperor lives in a state of exalted dignity which is almost seclusion. He meets his most influential subjects only rarely and in the most formal way. It would be surprising if he knew all of his Cabinet ministers even by sight. He does not go out into the world, yet he must know the world, and for those contacts which are indispensable for his Imperial function, he must rely on people who do have wide contacts and whose judgment he can trust.

The Lord Keeper's principal duties are "to keep the Imperial seal and the seal of state and to advise His Majesty and preside over the Court Councillors." The seal is the only legal signature in Japan. Without the Imperial seal or the seal of state the Emperor's assent has not been given to any law or ordinance. The Minister of the Household supervises the administration of the vast Imperial estates as well as the management of the palace affairs. The Grand Chamberlain is the titular head of the palace staff; the young officers tried to kill him in the 1936 mutiny, which shows that he was more than an Imperial major-domo; the last Grand Master of

Ceremonies had been Ambassador to London; he was a distinguished member of the so-called pro-British group and had very clear ideas on foreign policy. It is a suggestive fact that in all the rantings of the patriotic societies the "statesmen close to the Throne" are continually singled out for attack and are frequently the object of murderous plots and conspiracies. Since the present wave of aggression began in Manchuria in 1931, those statesmen have been publicly denounced by the patriotic societies and the young officers as their enemies, and in this suggestive fact we may see an indication of the atmosphere which prevails around the Emperor.

Those officials are not connected with the Cabinet and they do not change with changes of government. Their offices are in the palace; they are the Emperor's closest advisers; their position makes them his continuous confidants; they are his assistants in all his political work, his intermediaries in his dealings with Cabinet ministers and high officials. Through them or in their presence the Emperor is informed of all projects. Their unseen influence must be reckoned with in any description of the sources of policy. The most eminent Keeper of the Seal during the present reign was Count Makino. The general nature of his views may be inferred from the fact that there is no Japanese living whose life has been more often attempted by the reactionaries and Nazi-minded young officers. The present Lord Keeper is Marquis Kido. He was appointed by Prince Konoye; little is known of his views except that he belongs to the same school of political thinkers as Konoye. The Minister of the Household is Tsuneo

Matsudaira, who was a successful Ambassador at Washington and afterwards at London. He is no Fascist.

The influence of the Court group has been conservative and pacific. It rests on the power members of the group possess to see that policies recommended by the Cabinet and General Staff are scrutinized and examined in relation to the broad and permanent interests of the Empire as a whole. Their power, like the Emperor's, is diffused and negative, not direct and positive. They have walked these last ten years in daily fear of assassination by "patriots" who can get bombs and pistols from young officers. In their discreet way they have fought a long fight to restrain the army, but every time matters came to a crisis they have had to choose between mutiny and murder at home and aggression abroad, and they have chosen the latter. The advisers of a figurehead, however exalted he may be, are in no position to oppose policies backed by armed force and real power.

The Emperor plays his part in deep secrecy. He is the only ruler of a nation who has a private life today, the one national figure of the twentieth century who has no need of publicity. Yet enough is known of his personal character to justify the belief that he would have prevented the present war if he could. But with all Japanese, high and low, the spirit of the hive is stronger than individual will. When the swarm is buzzing, the queen bee must buzz too.

His subjects see little of Hirohito. When he leaves the palace, his crimson Rolls-Royce is surrounded by crimson motorcycles with armed gendarmes, and the streets are cleared to the depth of a block on each side of his route. He has never given an interview, never been photographed except formally, never laid a foundation stone, opened a bridge, or spoken into a microphone. Only once has he addressed a public meeting: on February 26, 1941, when he spoke to fifty thousand selected subjects gathered before the palace to celebrate the historically doubtful twenty-six-hundredth anniversary of his first ancestor. The other orators on that occasion were accommodated with microphones. The Emperor's voice could not be subjected to mechanical transmission. I watched and listened carefully; it was a chance in a lifetime. The Emperor, stocky and stout at the age of forty-one, was easy and confident on the platform; he has a good voice and he spoke clearly and well. Many of his adoring listeners would not even lift their eyes, but all could hear him. The occasion was, in its way, a test of personality, and the Emperor came through successfully. It was the only occasion on which his people, other than the highest officials, have been given an opportunity to hear the voice of the man who rules over them.

The Japanese do not discuss their Emperor, yet by piecing together scraps of evidence from men in a position to know, it is possible to form an idea of the character of the man who rules Japan.

It may be that the atmosphere of war and the pressure of his generals have changed his early disposition, but when he ascended the throne Hirohito was a man of peace. The name of his reign, "Showa," is written with two characters meaning "enlightenment" and "peace." He selected it himself. Statesmen who know him well have assured me that a love of peace was no form of words with Hirohito; it was a deep and steady impulse, and he hoped to leave as his record a reign unstained by bloodshed. But that was before the war.

"I believe the Emperor, at his age, to be as great a man as his famous grandfather, the Emperor Meiji, was at that age." This was the judgment of a great Japanese statesman, and it is the only personal opinion of the Emperor I have ever heard expressed by a responsible person whose impression had been formed at first hand.

What is known of his upbringing confirms the view that the Emperor is a peace-loving, modern-minded person. During the formative years of Hirohito's youth his father was a physical and mental invalid, secluded with his doctors and nurses. The young Prince was brought up by his mother, the Empress Dowager, a woman of spirit and character with broad interests. The "statesmen around the throne" at the time were Japanese of a type whose influence is extinct: cultured men with modern learning and a knowledge of the world beyond Japan. To finish his training, the Emperor, then Crown Prince, spent six months abroad. The patriots threatened to immolate themselves on the rails sooner than permit the Son of Heaven to leave the land of the gods. The Prince departed and no patriots were sacrificed under the wheels of his locomotive. He was a shy youth, speaking no English, and so nervous on his first night in Buckingham Palace that gray-bearded old King George went along to his bedroom after he had retired, tapped on the door, and chatted with him for a few minutes in a fatherly way to set him at ease. He returned to Japan with British ideas of mixing more freely with the people. To try these out a visit to a university was arranged and the students were told that ceremony would be waived. They passed from one extreme to the other, and the friendly mobbing that ensued was so embarrassing to the shy Prince that the experiment was not repeated. The Emperor sent his brother, Prince Chichibu, to Oxford. He enrolled as a student at Magdalen College and made English friendships which he still maintained until the eve of war.

The Emperor's human features are blurred by the veils that surround him, yet it can be seen that he is man as well as sacred symbol. He began his reign with high hopes and the ambition to continue the progress that Japan had begun in the reign of his famous grandfather. If he had succeeded he might have revivified the ancient monarchy and taken it into the modern age as a constitutional kingship in a liberal Empire. His young officers, who find words too weak to profess their loyalty, have defeated his ambitions. The Emperor of Japan is again a tribal figurehead, sitting silent and helpless like a wooden Buddha among the incense. It is a fair guess that he was one of the most miserable men in Asia on the night of December 7.

The second of the three major groups concerned in the making of Japanese policy is the Cabinet. The legal standing of the Cabinet is less important than the power it actually possesses to direct or influence policy. Its position a few years ago resembled, at a considerable distance, that of the British Cabinet. Its members were drawn from the various elements in the majority political party. The Cabinet focused the dominant opinion of parliament; through the Finance Minister and the Minister of Commerce and Industry it was in touch with finance and trade, and through the Minister of Agriculture and Fisheries with the rural communities. The Ministers of War and the Navy were the agents of their respective services, and the Foreign Minister was always a career diplomat. In the ten years before the Manchurian adventure (1931) the Cabinet was undoubtedly the government of Japan—a government handicapped by the independence and intransigence of the fighting services, but still the government.

The picture is not the same today; the present position of the Cabinet illustrates the changeable and unfinished state of the Japanese political structure. The elected element is at a very low ebb. There is no dominant party representing a majority of voters; there are no parties. The Cabinet has become a bureaucratic rather than a political institution. Its members convey the views of the various departments to the government and instruct the departments in the policy of the government. The Cabinet, however, is still a representative body; of its eleven members five are drawn from the fighting services.

Nowhere in the world has more parrot talk been heard about the inefficiency and the corruption of political parties and politicians than in Japan, and since the custom of selecting party leaders was abandoned, nowhere in the world has there been such a procession of incompetent mediocrities through the highest post of the Japanese Empire, the Prime Ministership. There has been but one exception, Prince Konoye. With the decay of the parties and the decline of representative government, the head of the Japanese Cabinet has come to resemble the Imperial chancellor in the old German regime rather than the British prime minister. He is not the Minister-President of a body representing a majority party, but the chief executive of government, selecting his colleagues for reasons that seem good to him, but not because of their political or party connections. Konoye is the embodiment of that change. He came nearer to being a real executive Prime Minister than any of his recent predecessors. Many of these were amateur statesmen selected from the army or navy or the bureaucracy. Their terms of office—one cannot say of power—were short; they were taken on trial and they lasted only a few months. Yet one ruling idea can be seen running through their shabby and ineffective history; the Emperor's advisers who selected them were persistently trying to exclude men of an extreme tendency. They realized the danger of the revolutionary forces which had twice broken out in assassination and mutiny. They were playing for time, hoping that gradually the fever would subside and the wild men be brought under control. This thoroughly Japanese policy regarded the young officers as erring children and not as enemies of the state, like the Communists. It has failed. The army and the navy and Nazified bureaucrats now rule Japan, and have staked its future on a war with the two nations which can hurt it most.

Konoye belongs to an old family of court nobles. Such ancestry has a significance which goes beyond the prestige of his aristocratic standing. The court nobles were those who remained with the Emperor while the military clans monopolized the Imperial authority. They, like the emperors, were reduced to impotence and poverty by the military clans. It cannot be imagined that the Imperial house and its immediate retainers have forgotten those humiliations. Somewhere in the background of Konoye's mind there must be an instinctive feeling that it is his duty to stand between the Emperor and the encroachments of the army. He admits, however, that the army occupies a peculiarly influential position. He said to me once:

"The Cabinet must work in harmony with the army, but co-operation with the army is not necessarily a military dictatorship. What our friends abroad have to remember is that we are Japanese and do things in a Japanese way. It is after all the Japanese army in the Japanese nation. The army is drawn from the whole manhood of the nation and is very close to the people. It would be quite impossible, according to Japanese ideas, that so large a part of the national family should not have an influence on our affairs."

Konoye has never been a member of any party; he wears no political label. He is not interested in abstract principles; he discusses political topics from the strictly practical point of view, not asking whether a certain policy will promote some ideal or other, but whether it can be helped, and what can be done. Deep down in his heart, as in every man's, there must be some cause, some thought, he would face a firing squad for, but he does not wear his heart on his sleeve. In quiet times he might not have been Prime Minister, but he is too intelligent to be an aristocratic idler. He was born in a political household; his father had political ambitions. He died while the present Prince was a schoolboy of thirteen, and Konoye afterwards spoke bitterly of the ingratitude of politicians. He said:

"While my father lived we had many friends, for

people came to see him from early morning till late at night. Very few came after he died. Men who had received favors from him seemed to have forgotten and there were some who demanded repayment of loans they had made to him. One, a wealthy politician, was particularly merciless. This bred in my youthful mind a tendency to defy injustice in the community. I was a gloomy youth with a tendency to read extremist literature."

His earliest impressions disposed him to dislike the political parties and their wealthy hangers-on. At the age of twenty-eight he was taken to the Versailles Peace Conference by Prince Saionji, Japan's titular chief delegate. Before going to Paris he published a dissertation setting forth the principles governing the peace and happiness of mankind. He advocated internal social reforms in order to guarantee greater justice among individuals and international reforms to assure equality of rights and opportunities among nations. Some eighteen years later when Colonel House published his views on redistribution of the world's resources, Konoye repeated at a private conference in Tokyo his own early opinions:

"New wine should not be put in old bottles and it is unwise to let it burst out of any bottle. To guard against this is the duty of statesmen. Evolution operates ceaselessly and brings about changes in the world quite apart from our designs. One of the most notable of such changes in recent years is the rapid movement forward of backward nations, approaching the level set by leading powers. This leveling movement should not be thwarted but properly guided. Great nations should be generous in this."

Here you can see the typical liberal, the typical moderate, hoping for peaceful change. It is significant that Konoye has been the only Premier of Japan in recent times who has been really popular with the mass of the people.

He says that his interests in life are politics and golf. When he began to take part in the proceedings of parliament as a hereditary peer, politics were a kind of sport. Occasionally his real political interests appeared. When Tokyo was seething with popular demonstrations demanding manhood suffrage, Konoye was one of those aristocrats who, like the English reform peers a century ago, exerted themselves to pass a popular measure which the majority of their class opposed. Manhood suffrage in the hands of a politically immature people like the Japanese was simply a toy which they cried for. Konoye had no illusions on the matter; he was not interested in votes for all, but he was concerned to prevent an internal conflict and ready to side with the underprivileged when social justice happened to be the way to social peace. His aim was peace, harmony, stability; he was a compromiser. He understands and practices the native Japanese way, the "family-council way," of handling internal disputes. If a headstrong brother demands that some particular course be followed and gets into an emotional condition in which he may do something rash if he is frustrated, the remedy is to let him have his way and trust to time and experience to bring him back to a calmer frame of mind.

When the assassinations of 1932 showed that the young officers were in a dangerous state of revolutionary unrest, the government adopted the army's foreign policy—aggression in Manchuria, defiance of the League, scrapping of treaties—while a moderate, non-party Prime Minister applied a sedative policy of masterly inactivity at home. It was not enough to satisfy the malcontents who wanted Fascism at home as well as aggression abroad, and a second and more deadly outbreak occurred, combining mutiny with murder. Konoye was asked to take the Prime Ministership. He refused and it was not until two more Prime Ministers had failed that he at last accepted the post. He had refused because he was convinced that the army must be satisfied before stability could be recovered. He had been in office only a few weeks when the China war began. Konoye cannot have been ignorant that it was an unnecessary war and he will not escape responsibility for it, but he thought war in China a lesser evil than mutiny and revolt in Japan, and he accepted the assurances of the generals who believed they could repeat on the plains of North China the victory Hindenburg had gained at Tannenberg and finish the war in six months. How those expectations were disappointed is a matter of history. A year later Konoye resigned, but his early role of a disinterested aristocrat interested in politics and golf was by then finished forever. The policy of appeasing the army had led the nation into the most dangerous crisis of its history. Konoye was the last ace of constitutional government. So when the army demanded an alliance with Germany and a Fascist structure at home, Konoye again came in and again he conceded the army's desires. When Hitler made his agreement with Stalin, Japan, with delays and reluctance, followed him. When, later, Hitler executed another double-cross and invaded Russia, Konoye dismissed the Foreign Minister who had made the treaty with Germany and the agreement with Russia and began negotiations with the United States. There can be no doubt that the Court collaborated with Konoye in the removal of Matsuoka and his extremist colleagues. But Court and Cabinet were impotent when at last the navy and army decided that they were strong enough to fight America, and the prolonged though feeble efforts of the Son of Heaven and his aristocratic Premier were brushed aside. Hirohito and Konoye took their places in history beside William II and Bethmann-Hollweg.

The other half of the policy Konoye accepted from the army was the so-called new structure at home. In so far as total mobilization of resources was necessary for the war in China, it was a military measure which any Japanese government, like any other government, must adopt in war time. But Konoye had another object in view. It had been in his mind for years before the China war began. He called it harmony between the high command and the Cabinet. He understood the weakness of the Japanese system and he hoped to create a strong central government by bringing the army into it. He wanted the army to take a share in the new structure, and the army preferred to retain its independence. Konoye's interest in the new structure immediately cooled. He took a number of generals and admirals into the Cabinet in what ordinarily would be civilian posts, but his object was simply a desire to strengthen the Cabinet by having in it men who would be able to enlist military support because of their connections in the services. It was a political expedient, not a solution.

To understand why a constitutional solution is needed, the position of the army, as the third of the groups which make Japanese policy, has to be explained. It seemed some years ago that the course of political evolution in Japan would trend towards the position found in other countries where the civil power is supreme. But the course of political development in Japan since the army launched its policy of expansion by force has gone in the other direction. The civil power has shriveled away, while that of the fighting services has increased. Instead of the army and navy being arms in the hands of the government, the civil administration is the servant of the fighting men.

The power of the army and navy is a kind of dictatorship. It is not a dictatorship on the Russian or German model, in which all the powers of the state are concentrated in the hands of a single agency.

The army did not run the government. It set the course of national policy but would not assume open responsibility. It was only after war with the United States had been determined on that a General from the active list was made Prime Minister. Konoye had allowed the army to make war on China; war with the United States was another thing. He would not face it, and the army at last had to place its own man at the head of the central government. The public knew almost nothing of its new Prime Minister. The name of Lieutenant-General Hideko Tojo meant no more to the newspaper-readers of Japan than the name of an unknown Major-General John Smith would mean to the public of the United States. That did not matter; it was the army, not the individual, that had taken over the highest executive post in the government.

Outstanding personalities are rare in the Japanese army. A dictatorship held in commission by a hierarchy does not require them, and would regard as an impertinence the intrusion of a leader who had started up the ladder of fame from a soap-box. "Japan needs no Hitlers or Mussolinis," General Araki said one day, and when I tactlessly asked: "Why?" he gave me a mystical explanation which baffled further inquiry. "What does a nation want with dictators," he said, "when it has the three Sacred Treasures?" These, acquired by each reigning Emperor on his accession, are the mirror of the Sun Goddess, signifying truth, the chaplet of jewels, signifying mercy, and the sword, signifying justice.

General and Baron Sadao Araki has too picturesque a mind to be a typical Japanese General, but from the correspondent's point of view he had the immense advantage of being vocal, indeed voluble. He was in his element on the platform; not for him the long scroll of ideographs monotonously unrolled; he strode to the front and orated. Nor did he need the stimulant of a cheering hall. Once he talked to the Supreme Military Council (a hard-boiled group of old generals) for four hours on the superiority of his method of controlling restless spirits by kindness.

During the troubled years, 1932 to 1936, when Japanese officers were organizing political murder and plotting *coups d'état*, General Araki became for the outside world the symbol and figurehead of this unrest. He was misjudged and overestimated. Araki was a rhetorician,

intoxicated and intoxicating others with the exuberance
of his verbosity, but he was never a plotter and he had
neither the mind nor the character for political calculation. The picture of Araki as potential military dictator of Japan was not, however, merely a "build-up." It
was believed by the young officers themselves and it
originated in the eloquent addresses Araki made when
president of the Staff College. That post gave him opportunities for expounding his ideas to young officers,
and as his faith in Japan's mission was of religious intensity and his power of exposition as vivid and versatile
as his own personality, his name was known in every
mess and he became the idol of the young officers.
When a group of lieutenants killed the Prime Minister
in May 1932, Araki was War Minister. He resigned in
obedience to the official code of responsibility, but his
designated successor, General Senjuro Hayashi, pointed
to the explosive temper of the army and told his colleagues that only Araki could calm the excited feelings
of the young officers. His advice was taken and Araki
was returned to the War Ministry.

The ideas which had captivated the young officers
were crude, but Araki could envelop them in rhetoric
which stirred all the latent chauvinism of the Japanese
mind and exalted it into a national duty. If not the in-
ventor, he was one of the first popularizers of the phrase
"Imperial Way," though his efforts to define the way
lacked precision. "The Imperial Way," he wrote, "is
the harmonious fusion of the true spirit underlying the
foundation of Japan with the great ideal of the Japanese
nation." To explain the foundation spirit of the Empire
he cited the example of the first Emperor who subju-

gated the original tribes and established Japanese rule and order and ownership in the land. The central idea was clear. The Imperial Way is followed when Japanese rule is extended. As to means: "The first Emperor established the Imperial army to extend the heavenly work. . . . We of the Imperial army are leaders in displaying the Imperial Way."

Thus was national expansion on the continent glorified and raised to a religious duty. The Japanese tendency to exalt the military profession was reinvigorated as Araki eloquently showed how conscription made every peasant lad a sharer in honors once reserved for the military caste:

"Our army is matchless in the world. It is at once an Imperial and a national army. Once warriors were a privileged class; conscription was the greatest reform in a thousand years; it abolished the samurai caste, and all became equal in rights. In other countries the army is controlled by the government, which is in the hands of the people. The Russian army could be called the army of the Communist Party. Our army is organized by the nation under the command of the Emperor and it is unique in the world."

The quotations are taken from a volume of Araki's speeches called "The Spirit of the Soldiers of Our Empire." The fervor with which he could use the tribal myths of the Japanese race to gild with a religious glow policies of sheer aggression is his claim to fame.

The "young officers," whose restlessness has been the "propelling force" of the army for ten years, are by the nature of things even more elusive of portrayal than the generals. Lieutenant-Colonel Kingoro Hashimoto, who has a natural talent for being seen, is a good exemplar of the movement. He was military attaché at Moscow and Ankara, and returned to Japan proclaiming his admiration of Mustapha Kemal and his antipathy to democracy in any form. He made his sympathy with the mutineers of 1936 so plain that he was retired in the mild purge that followed. He obtained funds somewhere and organized the Great Japan Youths' Society as "a patriotic unit in politics." It was not his first essay in political organization, for while serving on the General Staff he had promoted a society of young officers, the Sakura-kai, or Cherry Blossom Society, which became a link between the army and the Japanese thugs in Shanghai. He was recalled to the colors during the fighting in China and was in command of a battery on the day the U.S.S. *Panay* was sunk. While the airmen were bombing the American gunboat, Hashimoto shelled the British gunboat *Ladybird*. It may have been in consequence of American and British protests that Hashimoto was again returned to civil life. He resumed command of his young men and engaged in reactionary politics. He was selected as a member of the commission appointed by Prince Konoye to draft a Fascist constitution for the "new structure." In the discussions he advocated the abolition of private property. "All property in Japan," he declared, "should belong to the Emperor."

Another who should not be forgotten is Captain Amakasu, of the military police. At the time of the great earthquake in 1923 a Socialist writer named Osugi was in prison together with his "common-law wife" and her nephew, aged eleven. Amakasu, with a couple of soldiers, entered Osugi's cell, walked behind him where he sat at a table, suddenly gripped his neck in the angle of a strong arm, planted a knee in the middle of his back, and strangled him to death. The victim did not utter a sound. That murder finished, Amakasu proceeded to the cell where Osugi's wife was confined. She had not heard the murder next door, and received the Captain with a smile. He spoke a word or two, while maneuvering for position, but he did not catch her with the same skill as he had caught Osugi, and strangling her was a noisy affair. In a third cell was the nephew, a child of eleven. Terrified at the noises which his aunt made in dying, he screamed aloud, whereupon the Captain came in and, catching his throat in his strong hands, soon stopped that. Amakasu was tried, and every endeavor was made to saddle the two privates with the responsibility for murdering the child, but they would have none of it. The *Mainichi* newspaper said that the public regarded Amakasu as a national hero, but he was sentenced to a short term of imprisonment. His sentence was reduced while he was serving it, and he became chief of police in Manchukuo when that field of new careers was opened to military talents.

Then there were the two subalterns who, during the China campaign, equipped themselves with two-handed swords and made a wager as to which of them would first kill a hundred Chinese in the old-fashioned way. They soon made their hundred apiece, but the Chinese were then on the run after the capture of Shanghai and the sport was too easy. The wager was extended and the number was made two hundred and fifty. The Japanese newspapers treated it as a fine example of Bushido (the way of the warrior) and recorded its progress. While the numbers were still mounting, the press either became tired or, more probably, received a hint that it was not good publicity for an army which professed to be liberating China. It did not occur to anyone that a man with a sword cannot slay men who have rifles and cartridges. The two officers were simply murdering unarmed Chinese fugitives. Those human beasts were not typical of the Japanese officer; the army, however, did not repudiate them.

The legal basis of the army's power is the singularly privileged position given the army and navy in the constitution, and it is morally supported by an equally privileged position accorded to them in the minds of the people. The constitution provides that the Emperor as commander in chief shall be advised on military and naval matters not by the head of the government but by the heads of the fighting services—the Chiefs of the Army and Navy General Staffs and the War and Navy Ministers. Those high officers report to the Emperor directly on matters coming under the head of national defense; in such matters the supreme command is exercised by the Emperor not on the advice of the government but on that of the chiefs of the General Staffs. The Minister of War is not appointed by the Prime Minister but by the triumvirate which exercises the powers of the high command—that is, the Chief of the General Staff, the Inspector General of Military Training, and the Minister of War. He therefore helps to choose his own successor. The Minister of War must be a Lieutenant-General or General on the active list. The Minister of the Navy must be a Vice-Admiral or Admiral. The army can and at times does withdraw the

Minister of War from the administration, with the result that the government has to resign. It can and does refuse to allow a qualified officer to serve, with the result that a Prime Minister of whom it disapproves cannot be appointed. The Minister of War is an interlocking director; he is the army's agent in the Cabinet.

The constitution which created this situation provided a check on the army by placing financial power in the hands of the legislature. But that power is reduced by another regulation which provides that if the budget for the year fails to pass, the appropriations voted for the previous year shall automatically continue. It is further restricted by the practice of presenting military and naval five-year plans with continuing appropriations which, once voted, are thereafter beyond the control of the legislature. Finally, it is established that the size of the army and navy is part of the Imperial prerogative reserved by the constitution for the high command. The government cannot prevent any increase in the army or fleet which the fighting chiefs may think necessary. The position now established and accepted is that it is the business of the high command to decide what it wants and the business of the government is to decide how to get it. The financial control which the constitution provided thus has been whittled away; the government is free to choose whether to issue bonds or raise taxation, that is all.

The army did not have to organize itself for the capture of political power, for it was already a part of political power. In that balance of groups which governs Japan, the army is the strongest group. It does not need a political party in order to make its influence felt;

it is already in the habit of using that influence directly in the innermost center of government and the ultimate sources of national policy. It is not an instrument in the hands of the government; it is part of the government. Its power is assured by the constitution and guaranteed by the psychology of the Japanese people. From time to time high generals declare that they mean to get politics out of the army. They do not say that they mean to get the army out of politics. What they say is that in whatever concerns defense, the army by the strictest of logic has to dictate foreign policy and lay the course which industry and finance must follow.

The army's influence in relation to the administration is not like that of any other public department; it is comparable to that of the Nazi or Fascist or Communist Party, differing from these only in that it did not have to conduct a revolution in order to achieve power. No Fascist party has arisen in Japan, no Hitler or Mussolini was needed to capitalize the nationalist and authoritarian sentiment of the people, because that sentiment is already incarnated in the army.

The story of revolutionary unrest in the Japanese army is too long to be told here. It was a strange Oriental hybrid, product of the impact of Marxism upon militarism. Young officers who hated Communism because it was supposed to be democratic were drawn to state ownership because they saw there a means of countering the influence of the capitalists and of providing a "national defense state" with unlimited armaments for the vast Imperial mission of which they dreamed.

Prohibited books by pre-Nazi visionaries who anticipated in a remarkable way the doctrines of Hitler and

presented them in native Japanese form were circulated
in mimeographed copies among the young officers.
There are many empty hours in a young officer's life,
and provincial garrison towns are dull. The officers had
natural grounds for discontent. Before the restoration
the military class was the privileged class of the nation
and all officials of the country were drawn from it. The
samurai, or warriors, were the only gentlemen. The
restoration abolished their privileges. As trade expanded
and industry grew in the modernized Empire, the new
commercial classes became the fortunate people of the
country. With the granting of the constitution there
arose the politicians, and their influence increased so
rapidly that party government seemed to have been
successfully established on the basis of manhood suffrage and the ballot box.

It was not surprising that poorly paid soldiers should
become dissatisfied with the social order and should ask
if all was well in a nation where the once honored and
arrogant military class had been reduced to such a lowly
position. The large number of majors and colonels who
were doomed to retire in middle life with a pension
which provided a meager suburban existence could not
but contrast their lot with that of the colonels and
majors of industry, for whom there was no age limit
and whose income continued to grow as business expanded. The narrow education and restricted experience of the soldiers had confirmed their traditional
belief in the supreme importance of their profession and
it began to seem to them as if the glorious prospects of
the Imperial restoration had indeed been betrayed
somewhere. The proud and idle officer in his shabby

uniform, eating his regimental meals at the cost of a few cents a day, keeping his family in drab suburbs and sending his children to public schools, compared himself to the get-rich-quicks whose ostentation filled the gossip columns.

The prestige of the military class was on the wane. In some of the Tokyo universities there had been demonstrations against military training. Many signs indicated that the decline would continue and be accelerated. The Washington naval agreements had fixed the strength of the Japanese fleet at three fifths of that of the American fleet. This ratio was not only humiliating; it meant a closed career for many naval officers. The army also was experiencing lean times. Its numerical strength had been reduced by "liberal" governments interested in economy, and their instrument was an able and ambitious War Minister who aspired to be Prime Minister and was cultivating the politicians and capitalists, mistakenly assuming that they were the rising forces of Japan. The workman's problem of unemployment had infected the proud profession of the modern samurai. Clearly, in the eyes of the young officers, the guilt lay on statesmen who weakly followed the lead of the foreign democracies instead of using Japan's superior strength to establish the country in the overlordship of the weak nations of eastern Asia.

It is unnecessary to include the legislature in the groups that make Japanese policy. The constitution of Japan gave parliament a weapon, the control of finance, which in capable hands would have given it real power. The legislators were without vision or faith or courage, and their obsequious abdication at the summons of a sham patriotism was in keeping with their history.

Certain other groups of the national family—big business, finance, international trade—which could influence policy and had found their natural channel in the legislature, can also be omitted. These groups have had to fall in with the army and influence it so far as they could by making terms for their co-operation.

The delay between the signing of the alliance in Berlin and the outbreak of war was due in part to the nature of the Japanese system in which policy was the outcome of interplay between the Court, the Cabinet, and the fighting services. It was due in larger part to the fact that the navy was not sufficiently prepared and was not quite sure that it would survive a war with the United States and England, even with the advantage of a treacherous start. We may give the Emperor and his civilian counselors credit for disliking and fearing war. No credit is due them for moral courage. The Emperor's "divinity" has not saved him from becoming the puppet of the warrior clans like his ancestors. Japan has swung back eighty years and has become a streamlined, modern military government instead of an antiquated feudal military government.

CHAPTER V

HOW STRONG IS JAPAN?

A NEW method of classifying the nations recently appeared. Karl Marx invented it, and the Axis propaganda bureaus resurrected it. It divided the countries, as Marx had divided their citizens, into haves and have-nots, the implication being that the latter would be justified in trying to reverse the position by all and any means.

The new classification was impetuously adopted by the Japanese press. To describe that prosperous and expanding nation as a have-not was not even approximately true, but it made a plausible slogan. It will be shown that it was not the needs of the Japanese people but the wants of the army and navy that led the nation into one unnecessary war after another. The driving force of the movement, which ultimately got beyond all control and culminated in the attack on America, was the hunger of the fighting services to increase their war potential by acquiring control of the resources of one quarter of the globe.

An examination of Japan's economic and military circumstances reveals formidable strength, but it is mixed with formidable weaknesses like faults in a deposit of defective ore. Many observers saw only the weaknesses until the war burst on Pearl Harbor like a typhoon. Others were bemused by kindly sympathy towards a nation they envisaged as a poor and ugly new student struggling to get on in a cold world. The conception of Japan as weak and poor was useful to the Japanese militarists. It lulled the enemies they were preparing to fight into thinking that Japan could be defeated without war or rubbed out in short order. Like the German legend of encirclement, it formed the staple argument of the war budgeteers in Japan. It helped the fighting forces to destroy the incipient liberalism which was gradually growing and to replace it by a collective military dictatorship. By the all-inclusive General Mobilization Law it has converted Japanese industry into the arsenal of a "national defense state"—that is, a state whose primary function is war.

Whatever his position, even if he were a member of the Cabinet, nothing would surprise a civilian Japanese more than to be told anything tangible about the equipment, supplies, and reserves on which his fighting forces decided they could fight the United States and the British Empire. Such matters are "military secrets," the holy of holies, and no corner of the veil must be lifted. The complete facts are probably known to less than twenty men in Japan and a few in Germany. Instead of discussing Japan's strength and weakness in estimated figures which cannot be checked, let us look at the picture from the Japanese angle, study both sides of the façade, and see where the Japanese are conscious of weakness and where they have proved their strength. In the process it will appear how the army was able to control not only the government but the mind of the nation and work itself into the frame of mind where a fatal gamble comes to appear a short cut to paradise.

I. The Economic Position

What did the Japanese want? Was it true that their only choice lay between breaking into someone else's back garden and dying of saintly starvation in their own? Was the Japanese question one of a young and expanding nation overcrowded in its narrow homeland and debarred from the expansion that it needed?

Japan's foreign policy, it was said, was a diplomacy of necessity. She had to support a population half as large as that of the United States on an arable area half as large as California's. When Commodore Perry carried President Fillmore's message to the Tycoon eighty-eight years ago, Japan was a nation of farmers sustaining an upper crust of warriors. A bohemia of immortal artists supported itself in splendid poverty or ate the rice of wealthy patrons. There are more farmers in Japan today than there were then. The land is saturated and super-saturated with human labor; two million Japanese cultivators live on farms of less than one and a quarter acres; more than two thirds of all the farmers, whether proprietors or tenants, occupy holdings of less than two and a half acres. The average holding of each person working the land in the United States is 31.7 acres; in Japan 0.9 of one acre. The French peasant is thrifty, but the Japanese farmer has, on the average, less than one sixth of the land that the French peasant plows, and he has four or five children instead of the Frenchman's average of two. Fifty-three per cent of the population live on those tiny green farms, cultivated with an intensity which few Americans devote to their gardens.

The other half of Japan, the 47 per cent, lives by industry and foreign trade. Industry has provided an expanding frontier for the surplus labor of the farms. It has been the outlet for Japan's growing population and the safety valve of her social structure. It needs wide markets and cheap raw materials. The basic metals and materials on which modern industry is built are not found in Japan in adequate quantities. In recent years sixty per cent of the total bill paid by Japan for imports from abroad was spent on four primary industrial necessities: cotton, ores and metals, wool, oil. Those were in no sense luxury imports; they are necessary to subsistence, simply to keeping alive the Japanese people and providing them with food, clothing, and shelter.

Thanks to energetic capitalists and cheap labor, the Japanese scale of living became the highest in Asia, though it was still ultra-simple by American standards. The "poor working man" of these United States has no real notion of what poverty means. There are shacks in America, it is true, and too many of them. But they are the dwellings of the submerged fiftieth of the population; they are not the type of the American home, nor are rice and pickles, seasoned once a day with a scrap of salt fish and varied in the season by sweet potatoes, the normal diet of American laborers. The Japanese standard of living was rising steadily and relatively rapidly with the modernization of the country and the increase of production. It is now lower than it was fifty years ago. For that upper crust of two-sworded warriors which had become an idle effete privileged class in Perry's time has become a modern navy inferior only to America's, an army numbering more than a million men on active service, and a flying force of great though unknown strength. In America the wealth acquired by rising production went back into the pockets of the people, to be spent by them usefully, wastefully, charitably, extravagantly. Japan's rising wealth for the last ten years has gone into the pockets of government, to be spent on armaments.

Western observers of the Japanese scene who followed the rule of putting themselves in the other fellow's place found much that appealed to their sympathy and sense of justice. We had a picture of a nation of energetic and ambitious people overcrowded in their ancient homeland, debarred from the relief that emigration into countries already settled by other races could give, and restricted by tariffs and preferences and quotas from selling their manufactures freely in all markets. This was the situation, we are told, which determined Japan to obtain control of the natural resources of that part of the globe where the Japanese race belongs and where the white races have no permanent or indispensable interests.

The picture is an impressive one, but it contains contradictions which destroy it. The Japanese also claim that they have made unparalleled progress. Their superior development is one of the reasons put forward in support of their pretensions to take charge of eastern

Asia. The claim of superior development is well founded. No other nation in Asia and few anywhere are able to show such a growth of wealth and power as Japan has achieved within one lifetime. But how comes it that a nation so cribbed, cabined, and confined that it must expand or explode has made such progress? Even admitting that Japan started from zero and that all of us have progressed in the same period, there is a sharp contradiction between the plea of explosive poverty and the evidence of growing wealth.

Japanese who suppose that their Empire lacks colonies and oversea possessions can be recommended to study the map and re-read their own recent history. The area of Japan is 147,610 square miles. The annexation of Formosa, Korea, and South Sakhalin after the wars with China and Russia added 113,000. Manchuria, which in everything but name is a Japanese possession, brought the immense addition of 504,592 square miles. In the short space of forty years the territory which Japan owns or controls has expanded fivefold from 147,100 to 764,864 square miles. This does not take account of the mandated islands of the Pacific, some 2,400 in number, small in area, but strategically invaluable.

As we are discussing the case of a nation which says that it has no room to live, it is pertinent to ask how a population which had been stationary for two hundred and fifty years has latterly been advancing by leaps and bounds until Japan today maintains more than twice the population she was able to support half a century ago. Well-being also rose. The standard of comfort which the Japanese people enjoyed until the present China war began was the highest in Asia, and their opportunities of education and career were incomparably wider than those of their Asiatic neighbors.

Recently Japanese apologists have said that Ottawa agreements and quotas and exchange restrictions have radically changed the conditions in which Japanese prosperity was built up and that the developments of the last few years were the last straw that broke the camel's back and caused the Japanese army to head an uncontrollable national movement. Japan's official trade figures give the lie to those who say so. In 1935—the last year before the China war for which full figures are available—Japan's foreign trade was one hundred per cent greater than in 1931, when the depression was at its worst, and it was the best trading year in Japan's history. Her own records show that, apart from the great depression of ten years ago, Japan has never ceased to expand its productive power, its foreign markets, and the opportunities of gainful employment for its people. Japanese liners and freighters sailed every sea and the Nippon Yusen Kaisha (Japan Mail Steamship Company) was probably the most uniformly prosperous shipping enterprise in the world.

There was no serious food problem. While she was doubling her population Japan was simultaneously doubling her harvests. New Japan within her own islands grows approximately twice as much rice as old Japan did. The explanation is chemical fertilizer. Every country may justly demand the right to sufficient food for the needs of its population; but it would be clearly immoral for a country to extend its boundaries into its neighbor's territory under the plea of a search for food unless it had made the fullest use of its own resources and found them inadequate.

An accomplished biochemist, Dr. Egerton Charles Grey, spent a year (1927) in Japan investigating the food question for the League of Nations. His inquiry was conducted with official cognizance and assistance. For quantities he took the detailed reports of the Japanese Department of Agriculture; for quality he made four hundred analyses in a laboratory placed at his disposal by the Imperial Nutrition Institution of Japan. The results were different from what he expected. Taking first grains, the daily bread of life in every country, he found that the number of kilograms available annually per head of population in Japan was 217; in Great Britain it was 266; in Germany, 285; and in the United States, 372.

Allowance must be made for the fact that in the three last named countries the harvest has to maintain a much greater number of horses and cattle than Japan possesses, and also for the fact that while the weight of the average adult American man is around 150 pounds, the weight of the average Japanese man is about 110 pounds. Besides cereals, the Japanese also consumed other foods —vegetables, fish, fruit, sugar, and so on—amounting to 486 kilograms per head of population. "It cannot be claimed," says Dr. Grey, "that there is any shortage in the quantity of food in Japan when the government statistics show a daily supply of three pounds of food per head." In Britain a large proportion of the industrial output is needed to pay for imported food. Japan has had to import practically no food in normal years. Whatever conclusion we may reach regarding other materials, it is clear that even an effective blockade could not starve out the Japanese people. And the use of the word "effective" places a great strain on the imagination when it is applied to a country geographically situated like Japan.

While it is impossible for any Japanese to deny that his country has up till now been self-sufficient in food, it is equally impossible for anyone else to deny that Japan is deficient in basic raw materials. But when it is claimed that the situation leaves Japan no choice but to bring new productive regions under her control, we again encounter a contradiction. Only a few years ago Japan took the lead in the world's cotton trade away from England. This was accomplished without sending Japanese troops into the Southern states or obtaining any control of basic material other than may be exercised by a buyer who walks into the cotton exchange with a letter of credit in his pocket. Cotton is not the only landmark of Japan's industrial progress. There is not a market in the world where Japanese goods are not sold nor a country in the world which can show such a steady increase of gainful trade as Japan.

Japan started from zero in 1868, and comparisons based on a zero start are likely to be dramatic rather than informative. Let us leave out the adolescent years and take the adult years measured from the Russian war, which happens to be the middle point between the restoration and the present day. In 1904 Japan's foreign trade was worth 690,000,000 yen, equal to 14.63 yen per head of population. In 1937 that trade was worth 6,958,000,000 yen, equal to 95.41 yen per head. (During the years of stability, while the gold standard held good, the Japanese yen was worth fifty U.S. cents. In ten

years of continental aggression and armament extravagance it has sunk to half that amount.) How comes it,
we must again ask, that a country in Japan's supposedly
desperate predicament has been able to build up such
a flourishing foreign trade and increase it year by year?
Compare Japan to a young man entering the family
business; thirty-seven years later he is able to say that
the business is ten times bigger than it was when he
started. Could anyone in such a position declare that
he had been unjustly treated by society? Do we excuse
such a man for beginning a career of banditry on the
plea that he has never had a fair chance? Japan's record
in world trade is one of which any country would be
proud, and it shows that neither the handicaps nature
imposed upon Japan when she neglected to store iron,
coal, and oil under the Japanese hills or those invented
by man have prevented healthy development.

Only one conclusion can be drawn: the picture of
Japan as a nation deprived of living-room is not a description of an actual situation but a highly colored
anticipation of imaginary future troubles.

The structure of propaganda that has been crystallized in the phrase "haves" and "have-nots" proves
on examination to be a house of cards. On the record it
appears that the Japanese have been able to find raw
materials for their industry, and until the China war
had disorganized their finance they had no difficulty in
finding exchange with which to pay for them.

The attempt to justify Japanese aggression by economic determinism rests, like a quack advertisement,
on selected half-truths. The suggestion is created of a
poor country with few natural resources of its own,

inhabited by a growing and energetic nation impelled by irresistible forces within itself to seek in its neighbor's territory the necessities it cannot find in its own. It is, of course, true that Japan does not produce in her own islands everything she needs. What nation does? Japan does not possess the coal deposits that started England on the steam age any more than English fields grow the cotton that Lancashire spins or the United States the rubber on which its automobiles run. The fallacy in the argument is the suggestion that Japan has not been able to get what she needed. It has been shown from her own record that she has been able to double her population, elevate their standards of living, and build up a modern industry. Like other countries she has had to get her raw materials where they are produced, and she has not failed to get them. We must therefore decline to be moved by the unsubstantial complaint that the Japanese have been deprived of the opportunity to live and prosper.

II. The Military Position

It is not from the wants of the Japanese people that the pressure for aggression has come, but from the desires of the army and from the fact that by Japan's social ideas and political structure the army has the power to appropriate the bulk of the nation's productive capacity to its own uses and turn national policy into the channel it desired.

The argument that military insecurity finally drove the fighting services into irrepressible revolt is as fallacious as the argument of industrial insecurity. Would the Japanese navy and army be fighting America and

Britain now if they had lacked steel, oil, chemicals, rubber, aluminum, manganese, nickel, and the rest of the munitions materials? But the fear that economic disabilities might paralyze their arms was the strongest factor in the propaganda by which the fighting services worked themselves up to attack America and Britain, in whose political ideas they saw a perpetual challenge to their own policy of expansion by armed force.

Japan's military position was and is a mixture of strength and weakness. She has built up powerful forces, but her own territory does not produce in adequate quantity the essential materials needed by navies, armies, and air fleets. The situation in the Far East today follows the Japanese army's discovery that military power alone will not win modern war. The Continental policy of expansion into the mainland of Asia was at first inspired by the need for strategic or geographical security. The defeat of Russia in 1905, the expulsion of Russian influence from South Manchuria, and the annexation of Korea gave Japan security at the time, but victory was due to Russian weakness more than to Japanese strength. The army believed that Russia would seek revenge, and the agitation for larger forces began immediately after peace had been signed at Portsmouth, New Hampshire. The European war, the admission of Japan to the Supreme Council of the League of Nations, disarmament, and, above all, the Bolshevik Revolution thereafter combined to remove Japan's fear of Russia, but when it appeared that a new Russian state was arising, the army reverted to its old policy. The Manchurian adventure was carried through and the Japanese fighting frontier was advanced deep into Asia.

where the stronge:
sequences of sucl
action.

As in all great n
of aspiration, amb
den forces at worl
lutionary, half-ch:
cided with a moc
Japan had become
was necessarily acc
The Japanese are :
imitators and ofter
claim a unique gif
foreign things to J
thesis has consistec
tailor achieves whe
another. Japan tod:
complete down to
itism although the
Gentile, and that
being called imitat(

In the years of
when Wall Street
labor was going or
could be seen in J:
honors, the Japane
tional effort ever r(
and power of the
it was intensified
world. Having no |
needs of the mode
selves, the Japanese

By that time military ideas had been transformed by the lessons of the European war. The Japanese army had learned that military power is not measured by a nation's armed forces alone, but also by its industrial capacity and its command of essential materials. The objective of the Manchurian campaign was not only the geographical security to be achieved by moving the frontier so far north and west that the Maritime Province could be amputated and Russia cut off from access to the Pacific, but the greater military-economic security to be obtained from full control of Manchuria's unexploited reserves of ores and minerals.

Those unexploited reserves were playing a part in the army's thinking, of which the elderly generals and statesmen were ignorant. The young officers were determined that the new dominion they intended to create in Manchuria should not become what they called "a happy hunting ground for capitalists." They had felt the contagion of the post-war fevers; the instincts and passions released in Europe's depths by the collapse of Imperial Germany and Imperial Russia had affected them. Their native militarism and nationalism had met the impact of Marxism. The philosophy of the old German Jew who founded modern Socialism was congenial to and essentially akin to Japanese state-worship, and Marxism and Japanism fused into an Imperialist-Socialist amalgam which would have amazed Karl Marx. When a military and bureaucratic state adopts a policy of expansion by force, state Socialism is inevitable, call it the Imperial Way or the New Order or what you will. The historic Marxian formula: "state ownership and control of the means of production, dis-

tribution,
proletaria
thing whe
dow sold
surpassing

The co
accelerate
national a
of Nation
ment—in
means by
fighting.
"have" na
nots" suc

Before
no nation
Japan ha
plomacy
money m
the lack
tory. But
a nation
Manchur
tions, the
dilemma
give up t
to be thr
ployed.
their for
would g
be fed ar
be froze

ing America and Britain they had been copying the wrong models.

Some of their discontent was itself imitation. It echoed the criticism which ascribed all the ills of the day to the Versailles Treaty and ignored the ruinous effects of war, that elephantiasis of social diseases, upon an industrial civilization facing problems which only a long period of peace can solve. The young officers fell victims to political charlatans who dreamed of restoring a Japanese golden age which had never existed. Genuine idealists revolted against a form of civilization which produced a degraded proletariat, mushroom millionaires, and Tammany politicians. Western civilization seemed to be reproducing its degenerate progeny in Japan. Poverty-stricken farmers were selling their daughters to the Yoshiwaras that pullulate in every Japanese city and village; a new, "un-Japanese" proletariat was being infected with dangerous thoughts.

Japanese whose consciences were touched did not stop to reflect that some Japanese farmers had always sold their daughters, that actually poverty had diminished in Japan, and that the poorest Japanese today had greater freedoms and greater opportunities open to him than his progenitors had ever known. It did not occur to them that there might be a connection between the poverty of the people and the extravagance of the government in maintaining simultaneously a great conscript army and the third largest fighting fleet in the world. Jingo writers asked what Japan's army and navy were for if they could not enforce her own policy in Asia.

The equivocal cry "Back to Asia" was raised by na-

tionalist politicians who expounded army views. The Japanese people were told to return to "Japanism" and their own ancient civilization. Painted-up history, a raw inferiority complex, and the absence of a sense of humor combined to make the Japanese masses sore with a sense of unrecognized talents and frustrated destinies. The new movement drove out the incipient Communism which had begun to appear among the students and the factory workers. It drove out the anemic liberalism of the intellectuals. It found exponents among the rising politicians and it attracted the young and ambitious bureaucrats. Prince Konoye listened to it.

The House of Representatives in Tokyo heard one of its younger leaders declaim:

"Back to Asia has long been the motto of our party, by which we mean that we should part company with the materialistic civilization of the Occident which we have followed blindly for sixty years and return to the old spiritual life of Japan and preserve Asia in accordance with the pristine culture and ideals of the Orient. The state of European countries already indicates that the materialistic civilization of the West has entered upon a period of decadence. The unfortunate plight of our own country at the present moment may be traced to our unconditional surrender to Occidental civilization during many years past. If we should at this juncture boldly return to our ancient ways, solve all our problems in accordance with the old spirit of the East, and succeed thereby in establishing permanent peace in the Orient, it will not only bring happiness to the peoples of Asia but may give hints to the Western world for its regeneration."

The speech in which this passage occurred was one

of a kind that soon became stereotyped. It declared that the establishment of Manchukuo by Japan was not the end of a successful adventure but the first step along a new road to national greatness. The translation given here was made by a Japanese diplomat in strong sympathy with the views expressed, a sympathy he has been able to translate into policy. It is excellent, but the English words do not bring out tones which would be clear to Japanese readers. They would translate its thought as follows: "Let us cease following Britain and the United States. Let us return to our own ways and our own part of the world where we can solve all problems with the strong hand. No one can stop us."

Foreign governments treated the speech as a brilliant but irrelevant exercise.

The protagonists of expansion abroad and totalitarianism at home found a slogan which has never failed to arouse Japan's sentiment. It is a slogan as universal and as old as humanity. It ascribed all evils to foreign innovations and aroused the inherent nationalism of the mob with its false promise that all would be well if Japan would cast out those innovations. History was repeating itself. The Japanese restoration of last century was ushered in with shouts of "Restore the Emperor and expel the foreigner." Having accomplished their purpose, the victorious Imperialists promptly dropped their anti-foreign slogan, and the foreigners soon forgot it. To those Japanese who now wanted to drive out the incipient forms of democracy and the capitalism they disliked, the demand for a strong foreign policy was a weapon in their struggle to set up a Fascist state. To the army the Fascist state was indispensable for the expansion and aggression it desired. Both streams met in a movement beyond the control of the old bureaucrats.

The Japanese had sullenly accepted the decision of the American people which excluded them from the United States. That decision was humiliating, but it could not be disputed. Exclusion from the United States and the British Dominions seemed to justify the Japanese in turning their ambitions towards Asia. Eastern Asia was the line of least resistance.

In turning back to Asia, the Japanese were vividly conscious of their own history, and perhaps they expected that other nations would also remember it. By one of the most extraordinary decisions of an autocrat to which any race has ever submitted, the Japanese were locked within their own islands from 1637 to 1868. In those two hundred and thirty-one years the world of today took shape; the United States was founded and most of the fertile open spaces of the globe were colonized by Europeans. Had the Japanese not been forbidden by law to leave their own shores, they might have colonized the Pacific coasts of North America and acquired the Dutch East Indies. They could have established themselves in Siberia before the Russians came. The Rising Sun flag might have been floating over into Indo-China and Siam before Perry landed. The Japanese awoke in 1868 from their Rip van Winkle sleep to find the most desirable places in the world already occupied. Where could they satisfy their ambitions to be a great empire more easily than in China, huge, potentially rich, virtually unarmed?

In Japanese style, the movement found its leadership not in extraordinary personalities thrown up from the

depths but among army officers and government officials, all of them with careers to make, already en-
trenched in the seats of real power, working unseen,
like bees in a hive inspired by a common instinct and
purpose. Such a movement in such hands naturally did
not remain a campaign of slogans and agitation.

Officials, politicians, and staff officers studied the
political aspects of the problem. They found that Japan
had been enclosed within a diplomatic fence of treaties.
The Nine-Power Pact obligated Japan to respect Chinese sovereignty, to refrain from taking advantage of
the chaotic conditions created in China by revolution
and civil war, to seek no exclusive opportunities in Chinese territory, and to take no action without consulting
the other signatory powers. The naval-limitation agreements fixed the strength of the American, British, and
Japanese navies in a ratio of 10–10–6. The ratio was designed to preserve the peace of the Pacific by making
it impossible for any one of the three to attack any of
the others with any hope of success. It secured Japan
against aggression, and it gave her a guarantee that the
United States would not use its greater wealth and industrial resources to outbuild her. These were valuable
gains, but young officers saw in the inferior ratio only
another humiliation imposed upon their country. The
unthinking public were indignant against a diplomacy
which had accepted less than equality with America.
This indignation was a political instrument made to the
hands of those who wanted to change that diplomacy
and permeation of the navy and army by the same dis
content gave them a lever which could be used in the
inner machinery of government. To complete the

fence of legality within which Japanese expansionists were confined, there came finally the Kellogg Pact by which Japan pledged herself not to use force as an instrument of national policy. But if Japan was not to advance by the use of her superior strength, what were the army and navy for?

The policy of "Back to Asia" could not progress unless the treaties were destroyed. I quote again the words of the late Kaku Mori, a rising Japanese politician who had a remarkable discernment of the forces bearing Japan along: "The Japanese people are locked in their own territory by treaties. As long as the Nine-Power Treaty and the Anti-War Pact are construed in their present sense, Japan cannot expand in the Far East. If we are to progress we must break down this fence of treaties."

The Washington Conference had assumed that China was an organized state struggling to reconstruct itself and it proposed to preserve China for the Chinese by binding its members to non-interference while the internal struggle was going on. The Japanese militarists could never be satisfied with a policy that would permit the growth of a strong and independent and possibly hostile China. They asserted an interest overriding that of any other power, and they claimed the right not merely to intervene in protection of Japanese interests but to establish a suzerainty based on Japan's superior power. They demanded economic co-operation, by which they meant that China's potential resources should be exploited by Japan. China was to remain a producer of raw materials to be used for the increase of Japanese wealth.

Advocates of this policy described it as a Japanese Monroe Doctrine. It was Japan's mission, they said, to preserve the peace of Asia. Japan alone could effectively undertake that function because her powerful armies and fleets were on the spot. Rising politicians were turning their eyes towards Italy and Germany, where Mussolini and Hitler seemed to have found the way to a new social order where everybody would be in his place—the working man, the capitalist, the politician, and especially workmen of Leftist views and liberal politicians. Democracy was to them merely a mob; they preferred a hierarchy. And, to their thinking, Japan was destined by her superior strength, organization, and education to be the overlord of chaotic China and all the lesser peoples of east Asia. Those who wanted a Fascist revolution required the army's support at home and were prepared to endorse the army's adventures abroad in return for that support. There was no need of any bargain; the army also needed a totalitarian state and the political Fascists demanded expansion abroad.

The work of breaking down the fence of treaties began immediately after the last of them, the Kellogg Pact, had been signed by Japan and welcomed by the world's liberals with a chorus of futile praise. The first step was taken by the army. General Tanaka resigned from active service and became president of the majority party in the House of Representatives. It was publicly stated that he succeeded in doing this by means of a large "dowry" he had been allowed to draw from the money allocated to secret service during the Siberian expedition. The army has always played politics in Japan, but its game has varied with circumstances. In

1928 it financed a politically-minded General as leader of the majority party, a position which then carried the Prime Ministership.

General Tanaka began by summoning Japanese officials in China and Manchuria to what became known subsequently as the Far Eastern Conference. The conference was held "with a view to disposing of all pending questions between Japan and China by strong measures, since there was no prospect of settlement by the policy which the preceding Cabinet had adopted." That policy was one of patience and conciliation. It accepted the view that China's troubles were a temporary fever due to revolution and reconstruction, and it faithfully endeavored to carry out the foreign policies enjoined in the League Covenant, the Washington treaties and the Kellogg Pact. The Far Eastern Conference was immediately concerned with Manchuria. It held that Japan was responsible for the maintenance of peace in Manchuria because the first line of her national defense against Russia was there. The conference decided that if any opposition to Japanese policy arose, it should be met with force, no matter from what quarter it came—Russia, America, or England.

It was not known that the will of the League of Nations was unequal to its functions, and sanctions still seemed a formidable menace. Tanaka moved cautiously. A soldier of the old school, he recognized the strength of America and England, and a move was devised which they did not challenge. The war lord of Manchuria, old Chang Tso-lin, who had long had relations of mutual support with the Japanese army, had intervened in the Chinese civil war on his own account.

He had been defeated and his troops were retreating towards their home territory of Manchuria. Tanaka sent a small Japanese force into North China and issued a warning that Japan would not permit Chiang Kai-shek, the Chinese Generalissimo, to pursue Chang Tso-lin into Manchuria. The Chinese accepted the warning. The powers did not protest. In this smooth way Japan intervened in the capacity of protector of Manchuria and the first breach in the treaties was made. For the time that was all. Tanaka was the army's executive for its Manchurian policy, but he was a clumsy politician, and a technical blunder caused his downfall. A party Cabinet of liberal complexion succeeded him. Baron Shidehara, the Foreign Minister, continued his policy of patience and conciliation in China, and for three years more the spirit of the treaties prevailed.

The democracies were lulled into somnolence—if it can be said that the administrations of Baldwin and MacDonald in London and Hoover at Washington needed any lullaby. They seemed unaware that a breach had been made in the dikes their predecessors had built; Manchuria was a long way off. Hadn't the Japanese some rights there, anyhow? Looking on events in the Far East as "a fire on the other side of the river" from which they could easily isolate themselves, and absorbed in their own urgent industrial, social, and financial problems, the democracies continued to think of war as the people of Japan think about earthquakes. There is a really bad one only once every fifty years, they say; the last one is still too recent; there won't be another in our time. "Peace in our time," said Mr. Chamberlain when he came back from Munich. "Peace in our time," said the democracies when the Japanese made the first small hole in the Nine-Power Treaty, the legal instrument of peace in the Far East.

III. Government by Assassination

Meanwhile, hidden forces in the army were growing and gathering strength. The treaties finally crashed in a clap of thunder on the night of September 27, 1931, when the Japanese railway garrison in Manchuria marched out of its barracks and seized the country. This was the historic first occasion on which invasion was called an "incident." The government in Tokyo was kept in ignorance and its efforts to restrain the Manchurian army were contemptuously ignored. A few months later the government fell. It was the last majority-party government Japan was to know. Its successor lasted only a few months and collapsed when army and navy officers murdered the Prime Minister. The hidden forces had burst out into the open. The era of government by assassination had begun.

It was said that the army in Manchuria had run amuck. In a sense it was so; the army had taken the lead, defying the Cabinet and completely and finally destroying the policy of patience and conciliation. But as a Japanese statesman at the time observed, "How could a handful of soldiers have led seventy million Japanese by the nose had it not been that the soldiers' action touched a chord to which the whole nation was ready to respond?" The seizure of Manchuria was more than an act of piracy by an overseas army; it was something around which all Japan's pent-up national chauvinism at once rallied.

Thus it cannot be said that the economic and strategic factors which have been described were the cause of the present troubles. Rather might it be said that these furnished a method of rationalizing and justifying a course of aggression of which the ultimate causes lie deep in national psychology and are expressed in the national faith which worships the Japanese state and regards its head as divine. For many years enlightened civilian statesmen who knew something of the world and had the support of the throne had been able to hold the wild men in check. But the young officers had made a holocaust of liberal statesmen, and the Manchurian war had given the army the whip hand in government. The urge for armed expansion had at last arisen in irresistible form. Economic and strategic motives had been fused into one. New dominions oversea were sought not only because the homeland was deficient in natural resources but because an army with an aggressive policy needed control over the whole gamut of raw materials and the resources of huge territories.

Internal discontents had been rising against capitalism. They were now turned against liberalism because military expansion needed an authoritarian state organized for total war. The strongest element in the nation, the army, was the protagonist and driving force of the new policy. It came with terror in one hand and gifts in the other. Liberals went in fear of their lives. Army officers were attracted by the prospect of incessant activities and unlimited promotion. Capitalists were tempted by the opportunities of exploitation offered them. The people were flattered by a vision of their nation as overlord of east Asia. The adventurers and professional patriots who swarm in every community were lured by the prospects of easy wealth that would open when a near-by nation of four hundred million people was subjugated.

The aims of the movement crystallized in the demand that the Japanese people be given freedom for their activities in Asia. That platform was broad enough to hold them all. It appealed to old-fashioned soldiers with narrow ideas of strategic security and to new-fashioned soldiers with broad visions of illimitable resources made available for Japanese armaments. Young officials, chafing at their petty routine and meager future, were dazzled with the vista of unlimited opportunities that would be opened to them by the creation of a Japanese overlordship over one quarter of the earth. Every patriotic heart responded to those hopes of national greatness which the birth of the new Empire had awakened but which seemed too slow in coming to fruition. The initiative of the army had replaced the cautious control of the Cabinet and become the propelling force of Japanese policy. Aggressive imperialism had driven out peaceful penetration. By challenging an enemy whom the Japanese people had been taught to despise on an issue they thought vital to their national progress, the army made sure of a united front.

Those who sketched this program forgot that its execution would not be in the hands of a Bismarck, but of an army whose officers for the most part were as ignorant of the world as the peasants whom they led and whose narrow education in the military academy and staff college had but confirmed their naïve belief in Japan's Imperial mission. They convinced themselves that the motives of the new movement were patriotically pure and that the end would justify the means. But as has happened before, the means have shaped the end. The army found that Manchuria was insufficient. Defense of their gains required control of part of North China also, and North China's coal and iron were needed for totalitarian defense. The Chinese, who had submitted to the loss of the three eastern provinces, defended the ancient territory of China proper. The war that followed is not yet won. The Japanese idealists sought, if one takes them at their word, a China that would be friendly after being taught a short, sharp lesson, as Austria was friendly to Germany after the war of 1866. Their hope was destroyed by the means employed, and the savagery of the Japanese soldiers has sown a hatred which has passed into the life-blood of renascent China and has summoned onto the Far Eastern stage not the New Order of which the Japanese dreamed but a fierce nationalism which they have provided the enemy with, needed to sting and lash it into strength. The Japanese complained of encirclement. By their own doing they are indeed encircled, not only by the Anglo-Saxon democracies so long distant and indifferent, but by the Asiatic nations whom they have taught to fear and hate them.

CHAPTER VI

HOW WE CAN DEFEAT JAPAN

We assumed that if Hitler was defeated in Europe the Japanese would find themselves out on a limb in Asia. We assumed that their policy of fence-sitting was inspired by a desire not to be too tightly tied up with the losing side. We assumed that once Germany had lost the war in Europe, Japan would have to capitulate to the democracies, who would be in a warlike mood, fully mobilized, commanding the greatest fleets ever launched, and in undisputed control of all the important communication routes and sources of raw materials and markets in the world. We made no secret of our intention to "clean up" Hitler's little yellow partner as soon as we had finished Hitler. We assumed Japan to be an Oriental Italy with no future—jackal in the fight, puppet and vassal if the result was German victory. We anticipated no trouble in reducing Japan if the Axis met defeat.

Some of our assumptions were correct. The Japanese knew they were out on a limb. They foresee that Germany can be defeated; they do not regard themselves as Hitler's jackals and they consider Italy a third-rate power. They are in the war for their own interests. Their plan is to invade and conquer the western Pacific while America and England are battling Hitler. The Netherlands East Indies are the world's richest colonial estate. They produce oil, rubber, bauxite, tin, nickel, sugar, tobacco, fiber, palm oil, and other indispensable materials for war and peace. Their population of sixty million people offers a valuable monopoly market for Japan's manufactures. Holland won this rich estate by sea power three centuries ago. The Japanese propose to take it from them by air power. They intend to overrun and capture that region, to make themselves immune from blockade by its resources (which they will at the same time deny to their enemies), and to dig in so deeply while the Axis still is able to absorb the whole of Britain's and part of America's fighting power that a second great war will be needed to dig them out.

The adventure is an insurance against German defeat more than a gamble on German victory. The Japanese are attempting to protect themselves by taking up a position from which they believe they cannot be dislodged. The Japanese Empire would not be staked on any consideration other than the belief of the fighting forces that they could themselves answer for its safety.

It would be a reasonable calculation on their part, however, to assume that if the United States diverts a large part of its power to the Pacific, Hitler may get off with a draw in Europe. They would reckon a draw in

Europe a draw everywhere. If Hitler fails to make a draw of it in Europe, Japan's position becomes enormously more difficult. For "difficult" we who are fighting them say "impossible." But to understand their actions we must look at them through Japanese eyes fitted with Japanese spectacles.

They have never understood American psychology. They think democracies are constitutionally "soft." That a nation can be pleasure-loving, extravagant, forever running after novelties, pacific, loathing war; that an unbridled press, radio, and cinema may ceaselessly reflect and magnify all these things; and yet that such a nation may be revengeful and "tough" is something the narrow Japanese military mind does not comprehend. It expects that after defeating Germany the democracies will be tired, eager for peace, lower taxes, and normal life. It hopes that they will not face another stretch of war years to restore the *status quo ante* in the South Seas. It reckons that if they do, Japan can fight them off for a long time.

When Hitler's defeat is definitely registered, voices will be heard from Japan which have lately been silent. The graduates of American universities, the converts of American missionaries, the beneficiaries of American philanthropy will again proclaim that there is no country Japan would sooner be friends with than the United States. The missionaries who were thrown out will be invited to return and they may even get back control of hospitals and colleges that would never have existed without American charity. There will be domestic agitation against the Japanese militarists, and a good deal of it will be sincere. Parliament will be given its tongue again. It will be discovered that Japan's aims were purely economic; that she had no political or territorial ambitions anywhere. It will be said that with Japan strong and satisfied, peace in the Pacific is secure and Japan will gladly co-operate in its maintenance. All this will be offered to America as an alternative to a long and exhausting war. It is possible that Japan's military thinkers expect a rebirth of American isolationism. Judging by the space they received in the Tokyo press, many simple Japanese newspaper-readers must have thought that Senator Wheeler and Colonel Lindbergh were powerful men.

History repeats itself—not in situations which change with circumstances, but because character repeats itself. The qualities, the inner forces, that impel a man or a nation to act in a particular way in a crisis will make their power felt again when new crises impose new tests. We look to a nation's history for some knowledge of what it is likely to do under strain, just as we refer to a man's record and character.

Japan shut itself off from the world for two hundred and thirty-one years. No despot could have done that if the nation had not been willing to be shut up. When Japan in 1854 signed its first treaty with the United States, it threw off seclusion and, like most nations in a state of revolutionary emotion, it thought it had thrown it off forever. But action and reaction follow each other. Japan also threw off military government, but the wheel has come round again to military government, and Japan's recent policy reveals a revival of a deep national urge to be again shut up and secluded.

There seems to be a subconscious feeling that many

of the distinguishing features of Japanese civilization cannot survive contact with the world. The Sun Goddess, the Shinto mythology, the Emperor's divine descent, the uniqueness of Japan, the Imperial Way, the fables that are taught as national history—these are the things that make the Japanese pulse beat faster, and all of them suffer change and decay when the skeptical air of the modern world touches them. The Japanese mind is uncomfortable in the new world of Western free thought. As the Japanese big-business man goes home from his office at night and tries to lose his modern self in the tea ceremony—a ritual of barren and fantastic politeness—so the race seems impelled by its character to seek another era of seclusion. As it cannot live in its narrow islands, it gropes and fights for a larger home, a self-sufficing region where the riches of the tropics and the man-power of Greater East Asia shall guarantee security and even luxury, and where none can question the superiority and supremacy of the Oriental master race and its cherished myths and foibles.

At first it was supposed that control of China and Manchuria would give Japan the private *Lebensraum* she wanted, and army policy down to the time when Hitler made his pact with Stalin regarded Russia as enemy Number One. In 1938 Admiral Nobumasa Suetsugu wrote: "If China and Siberia are stabilized, Japan need not worry about food, clothing, and necessities. Germany's fate (in 1918) will never be ours." The success of Hitler's blitzkrieg in Europe broadened the picture. Indo-China fell like a ripe fruit and the Dutch East Indies became a prize to be gained in short order by the strong hand instead of by commercial penetration and boring from within. One fourth of the world was to be "stabilized."

Once before Japan has fought a "white" power. In its beginning the war with Russia resembled the war with America as a tiger cub resembles a tiger. In Pearl Harbor in 1941 as at Port Arthur in 1904 Japan snatched a start which she expected would win the race. The attacks of December 8, 1941 were intended to give Japan sea and air mastery in the western Pacific while she seized the British and American bases which she must immobilize if she is to invade the Dutch East Indies and plant the Rising Sun flag over "Greater" East Asia.

Japan had many advantages in her war with Russia which she does not enjoy today. The greatest of all revolutions was then kicking in the womb. A Japanese general was sent to a Balkan city where with unlimited funds he fed revolt in Russia. His role was disclosed after his death a few years ago. The Russians were fighting at the end of a single line six thousand miles long, and they could never adequately supply or reinforce their troops. Japan had the financial and moral support of Britain and the United States. A new nation, she was regarded as the promising pioneer of a new East.

When the war ended, Japan was exhausted. She had shot her bolt. Theodore Roosevelt was given a hint that mediation would be welcome. Russia was in no condition to refuse it. But the Russians declined to pay an indemnity and Japan did not dare to insist.

In repeating their opening move did the Japanese calculate that, at worst, they could repeat the close? They had fought themselves to a standstill, but they had taken a grip of Korea and South Manchuria, the first stepping-stones to their self-appointed destiny to rule east Asia. So in the present case they expect that at the end they may be left with the foundations of hegemony in the Pacific securely laid.

Japan will eventually be defeated by the Fabian method. That word does not mean slowness only. Fabius Cunctator was slow, but what he said was: "We can save the state by taking thought." The defeat of Japan will be a long process, but it can be expedited by taking thought. That means, to begin with, realizing the true dimensions of the problem the Japanese have set us, getting rid of our illusions, and trying, so far as we can, to enter into the Japanese military mind. There are men in the State Department and in the United States Embassy at Tokyo who have a good notion of how that mind works.

The Japanese Naval General Staff has checked and re-checked all its calculations of the military problems. Every detail that could be foreseen, every development that could be imagined, have been provided for. Their plans are as complete as such plans can be. But wars are not won by plans alone. In the end it is mind against mind, will against will. The ultimate blunders in any situation are psychological. The Japanese military mind, now dominant in Japan, does not understand the American mind. A true sense of American psychology would have saved the Japanese army from some earlier illusions. The Emperor's Rescript, the speeches of Konoye and other leaders, and the universal tone of the Japanese press prove that the Japanese believed that by making an alliance with Hitler they would inhibit the United States from continuing to assist Britain.

Psychological rather than strategical myopia is the fatal Japanese handicap; after all the intensive studies Japanese military men have made of China in the last twenty years, they do not understand the Chinese. All their original ideas about China have broken down; they have not learned the lesson; instead of seeing their mistakes they laid the blame for their failure on the trickle of assistance the United States and Britain have been sending to China. They misunderstood every aspect of the problem of China except the narrow military aspect. They reduced a complex political question to a simple military one. The only factors they saw were Japan's disciplined soldiers, professional officers, superior training, mechanical equipment. Against China's half-equipped and poorly trained troops a Japanese military victory was a sure thing. But military victory was only to be the easy prelude to a difficult political task. The Japanese generals forgot Bismarck's remark: "You can do anything with bayonets but sit on them." After five years of continuous military successes the Japanese in occupied China are still "sitting on bayonets."

The military minds which began the China war rule Japan. They are unconscious of their blind spots. Their science of war is a combination of Clausewitz for doctrine and the Battle of the Mazurian Lakes for strategy and tactics. This Prussian teaching they apply to a groundwork of the principles of Chinese classical military writers, with whose minds they have the affinity of a common culture. Oriental strategy stresses the value of stratagem and treachery. There are some Japanese who believe that the incurable kink in the minds of Japanese officers has been made by the Military Academy's teaching on the necessity of deceiving your enemy. They attach the greatest importance to the first treacherous thrust. It is minutely prepared and secrecy is absolute. The records of the Russian war and the China war do not show that Japanese military science has any surprises after the first. They follow the sudden opening move with heavy orthodox blows. Their plans are good, and they sacrifice cannon fodder relentlessly. They are poor improvisers. The Japanese habit of regulating action by precedent is deep-rooted. There are rules for the simplest actions. Even when these are applied to native customs which the Japanese naturally understand, they show inability to get away from the formula. In unfamiliar situations, such as a breakdown of novel machinery, the Japanese think slowly, and impassivity is the mask of a confused but disciplined mind. If the plan goes wrong, all is wrong. They are faithful unto death to rules and orders, but lost in situations for which new rules have to be invented on the spur of the moment. The only "spur" which "the moment" brings to the Japanese mind is the instinct to die. In battle that may save the situation, or it may seal it down in *rigor mortis*. It is usually all that they can do.

Speculation is speculation; armchair strategy is armchair strategy. The plan for victory will be worked out by the United States General Staffs in combination with those of their British and Dutch allies. Realism might begin by dropping the fiction that China can give us substantial military help at present. Chiang Kai-shek is pinned in his remote northern hinterland by superior Japanese forces. He cannot defeat them until he gets the planes, tanks, and guns needed. This does not minimize his heroism or the strength of his resistance. It has been a magnificent feat, but it has consisted in harassing the Japanese army along their extended lines and refusing them the orderly occupation in which they could sit down and exploit their gains. Later, when the Japanese line begins to sag and break everywhere, it will break in China also.

But it is America that has to defeat Japan in the Pacific. In that task the United States commanders have the use of the British and Dutch bases—so long as they remain British and Dutch—the active co-operation of considerable allied forces, including a new Indian army which may number nearly a million men drawn from fighting races and trained by modern methods. They will be supported by the whole power of those two glorious little democracies, Australia and New Zealand. Canada's role will continue to be played mainly in the Atlantic and in military aid to Britain. The A B D general staffs—America being the predominant partner—will make the plans. But America's unique and overwhelming power is that of her inventors and engineers. It is not rhetoric or boasting to say with me (not an American) that there is nothing like it in the world. Japan's yearly output of 8,000,000 tons of steel compared with the 88,000,000 tons which American mills produce is a typical and by no means exceptional example of the difference between Japan and the United States in military potential. American production lines will make bigger and better planes, more heavily armored, geared to new velocities, and gunned to new volumes of death-dealing power. There will be setbacks and successes. The war in the Pacific will be tedious; radio's appetite to interrupt its programs with exciting spot news will go unsatisfied for months at a time; yet tedium will be diversified by spurts and adventures devised by the inventive spirit of America to cheer our side and rattle the enemy. We should not expect that any Napoleonic short cuts to victory will be found. The development of high pressure over an enormous area will naturally be a slow process, and at the beginning more haste will be less speed. Victory will come from the irresistible pressure of superior power.

A NOTE ON THE *Type*

IN WHICH THIS BOOK IS SET

This book was set on the Linotype in Janson, a recutting made direct from the type cast from matrices made by Anton Janson some time between 1660 and 1687.

Of Janson's origin nothing is known. He may have been a relative of Justus Janson, a printer of Danish birth who practised in Leipzig from 1614 to 1635. Some time between 1657 and 1668 Anton Janson, a punch-cutter and type-founder, bought from the Leipzig printer Johann Erich Hahn the type-foundry which had formerly been a part of the printing house of M. Friedrich Lankisch. Janson's types were first shown in a specimen sheet issued at Leipzig about 1675. Janson's successor, and perhaps his son-in-law, Johann Karl Edling, issued a specimen sheet of Janson types in 1689.

COMPOSED, PRINTED, AND BOUND
BY H. WOLFF, NEW YORK